THINK ABOUT IT...

...by the time you retire from work, you will have spent approximately 90,000 hours in the workplace. Also, at the same time you retire if you attended church regularly during those years, you will have spent approximately 5,000 hours in church. This means for every 1 hour you spend at church you will spend 18 hours in your workplace. Yet for many Christians the workplace is a spiritual wasteland, a place to earn income...but not a place where they experience God's presence working through them while on the job. **When God Shows Up at Work** takes the reader from a definition of work through God's eyes and words to practical ways and real life stories of God working through His people in the workplace.

"I got this book given as a gift and I love it! I am a Christian who works in the aluminum business and want my workplace not just to be a place where I earn money, but instead where I can shine the light of Christ. So I was utterly delighted to receive a book which addresses the issues related to work and how to bring God's Kingdom into this, when God indeed shows up at work. This book also challenges me to use the time wisely and intentionally. Paul Curtas has not only written well, but engages with the reader...Very worthwhile!"

Evi Rodemann, Director, Mission-Net Europe

"This book is a masterpiece of Biblical reflection on the real life practical demonstration of how the Christian believer should practice their faith in Jesus Christ in the workplace. Paul uses real life examples from his experience and teachings from the Bible to help bring to life scriptural truth. I read the entire book cover to cover and enjoyed every chapter. I pray that every believer will read and apply the eternal truths contained in this book. I also pray that employers wanting to improve the employee relations in their company will read and apply these teachings in their place of work."

Chester R. Cook, Guest Relations Manager, Atlanta International Airport

"Amazing... As an administrator and teacher I have truly enjoyed this book. I loved it so much... that we are now teaching it to our Senior and Junior Class at our Christian School."

Rebecca McKeen, Administrator/Teacher, Grace Christian School

"Paul Curtas does an amazing job of helping our students see how their relationship with Jesus and work intersect. It is not only the students that are impacted. As someone that teaches business from a biblical worldview, Mr. Curtas has challenged and deepened my understanding of what it means to be a Christian in business. He demolishes the sacred/secular divide and demonstrates how God can use believers in the work force to be a light. He shatters the idea that there is a hierarchy to vocations, explaining that we can honor the Lord in whatever we do."

Amy DuBois, Faculty-BOL, Columbia International University

PAUL M. CURTAS

WHEN GOD SHOWS UP AT WORK

© **2013 by Paul M. Curtas**
Second Edition (October 2015) includes Chapter Discussion Questions
Current Printing (January 2018) Business Graphics, Knoxville, TN

"When God Shows Up At Work" is available in eBook format on
Amazon. The book is also available in German, (Spanish translation
coming in 2018). For more information go to *Godinwork.com*

ISBN: 978-0-9910729-1-0

Printed in the United States of America

Contents

Preface

Section 1

Developing A God-Sized View Of Work

Section 2

Defining Workplace Ministry

Section 3

Responding To Workplace Conditions

Section 4

Being The Church In The Workplace

PREFACE

WHAT YOU SHOULD KNOW

Many Christians walk into their workplace every day without giving much thought about God's presence there. Most would tell you that God is present everywhere, but with the many challenges and difficulties within the work setting they often have a hard time connecting God's presence to their workplace. For a long time, I had assumed that this was understood among most Christians because of the example of my mother and father. My father, who was a businessman all his adult life, started a manufacturing business in the 1960's. His understanding of God's presence in his work was evident in his business life. As a teenager I had the privilege of working among his employees. It was there that I first saw, through my young eyes, the importance of what it means to be a Christian in the workplace environment.

Early on my journey took me in pursuit of schooling for vocational ministry but along the way I found myself at times working in different jobs. In each of these I enjoyed looking for opportunities to engage my faith with those around me. I had worked over 15 years in vocational ministry within the local church setting, when I became General Director of the Fellowship of Christian Airline Personnel (FCAP) in October 1992. It was at this time that the importance of the Christian faith being engaged within the workplace setting was reinforced to me again. The journey has been revealing and enriching, as I have had the privilege of interacting with God's people and watching them in their workplace. Much of the materials collected for this book come from their lives.

My work in FCAP has afforded me the wonderful opportunity of working closely with people from North and South America, Europe, Asia, Africa and South Pacific. My travels have taken me among people into a variety of work settings around the world. It was early on that I noticed some characteristics in the lives of those who brought a spiritual influence to their work. They did not necessarily have fewer problems than others, often the same and sometimes even more. However, they clearly understood how God viewed their work and how their faith in Him related to the details of their work.

Though many, but not all of the stories in this book, are related from the airline context, the principles and characteristics they convey are not unique to the airline workplace, they are universal and apply to Christians in most any workplace.

The material before you comes as a result of my time interacting with people in the workplace for over two decades, and my studies of Scripture over the years. The book is divided into four sections, which embody four vital characteristics that I saw among Christians whose spiritual life and influence were obvious in the workplace. The first section stresses the importance of understanding God's view of our work and how it should influence our work every day. The second section defines and describes ministry with reference to the workplace; what it is and what it is not, and my involvement in it. The third section focuses on some of the pressures of the workplace and how we should be responding to these conditions in God's way. The fourth section summarizes the importance of Christians connecting together in the workplace and how it makes the church uniquely alive there and gives God greater exposure.

I have chosen to title the book, WHEN GOD SHOWS UP AT WORK, because it represents what I have seen through the lives of God's people in the workplace and what I have learned from Scripture. When God shows up in the workplace He does so mostly through His people. I trust that God will use this book in your life to give you a greater awareness and appreciation of how He can show up in your workplace.

ACKNOWLEDGEMENT

This book would not have been possible if it were not for God providing His people and resources. Though all of our thanks starts and finishes with God, I would like to acknowledge and thank those whom God provided along the way.

I am eternally grateful to God for providing my dear wife, Claudette, who is a partner in life and ministry and a blessing to me in so many ways. Her persistent labor of love in helping me with the revisions, as well as her insights and encouragement were of the greatest value to me. God also blessed me with Pat Lee, a retired English teacher/professor, whose creativity and expertise in English was both a huge help and a great inspiration. She encouraged me to stay the course while challenging me along the way. Next, I am thankful for Cristian Rusch, Tim Files, Landra Chasteen, Scott Bowman, Joe Ivey and Jim Rose, who read and critiqued the manuscript. Their suggestions and insights guided me along the way. Lastly, I want to thank God for the FCAP Staff and Board of Directors, for their patience and support as they watched this unfold over the last decade.

This book is dedicated to the Lord of the workplace and to the men and women whose resolute trust in Him shines brightly every day there. My humble prayer is that God would use the content of this book to awaken His people and bring His glory and influence into the workplaces throughout the world.

SECTION 1

Developing a
GOD-SIZED
View of Work

WHEN
GOD
SHOWS UP AT
WORK

1

GOD-SIZED
VIEW OF WORK

For more than two decades I have been privileged to be a part of the Fellowship of Christian Airline Personnel (FCAP). We regularly offer a two day basic training seminar which emphasizes the Christian understanding of God's perspective of work. The goal is to help employees understand how they can prepare themselves for the unique opportunities to minister which are inherent at their workplace. At one of these seminars an incident occurred which is particularly noteworthy. At the end of a session entitled "Developing a God-Sized View of Work" a woman with more than 25 years as a flight attendant began quietly weeping. Because we work in small groups at these seminars everyone was noticeably concerned. Seeking not to embarrass her, I asked if she would appreciate prayer. She answered, "Yes", but went on to explain her sorrow. She related that though she had been a Christian for years, she had no prior understanding of God's view of work or His perspective of it. She felt she had worked all these years with a view of work no different than non-believers. That feeling brought her overwhelming sadness.

From experience I have noticed that many Christians walk into their workplace every day with the purpose of their work defined exclusively by their company. They see little or no relationship between God and their work or the circumstances at their workplace. Some may see this relationship to mean that it is their Christian duty to do a good and honest day's work for a paycheck and then leave to enjoy the Lord elsewhere. Seldom do they give much thought that the Lord, who is ever-present, is actively involved in their workplace and is their supreme boss. The flight attendant of 25 years cried, not because she was a bad employee who may have stolen time from the company or had done anything else against company policy; but because she recognized that her work was practically a spiritual desert. She seemed to do her work for no better reason than anyone else around her.

Think about it! By the time you retire... how would you describe the years spent in your workplace? Would you see them as a spiritual wasteland or a spiritual harvest field? It is estimated that by the time you reach retirement you'll have spent over 90,000 hours in the workplace. Also, by the time you retire, if you attended church regularly, you'll have only spent approximately 5,000 hours at church. Many Christians cannot experience the joy of understanding the pleasure of God's purpose and presence in their work simply because they don't know He is there. In some way we have been deceived to believe that the purpose and presence of God is to be found somewhere else other than the workplace. Why? Because many Christians believe there is just too much chaos and too many problems to experience God's presence in such a place.

Take a moment to recall one character in the Bible who impressed you. The setting of the story is most probably in the world amidst chaos and adversity. Most of the stories in the Bible find God working on behalf of His people in a world surrounded by people who both oppose God, yet need God.

In 2 Corinthians 2:12-14 Paul tells of an open door to share the Gospel in the town of Troas. He was supposed to meet Titus there, a friend and partner, who did not show up. With deep concern, Paul eventually decided to move on to the next rendezvous point. Paul took this opportunity to share an incredible truth as to how he understood God's presence and purpose in every place. In verse 14 he says *"But thanks be to God, who always leads us in His triumph in Christ, and manifests through us the sweet aroma of the knowledge of Him in every place."* Did you notice? He did not say that you need to be in the right place at the right time to experience God's presence; nor do you need somehow to look for God's activity and in some way attach yourself to it. The truth is...God wants to show us He is triumphant through us personally in all of life's circumstances to spread the aroma of the knowledge of Christ through us in "EVERY PLACE." This includes our workplace! This is crucial, as we will spend a major portion of our lives at work.

But unfortunately, we have become selective as to where we think God should be enjoyed. Many churches these days are spending millions of dollars to provide comfortable places for our faith to shine for a few hours. At the same time we have grown cold toward God in places like work because we don't see Him as being active there. In his book, *"A Taste of New Wine"*, Keith Miller exposes this kind of thinking.

> It has never ceased to amaze me that we Christians have developed a kind of selective vision that allows us to be deeply and sincerely involved in worship and church activities and yet almost totally unchanged in the day-in, day-out guts of our business lives...and never realize it.[1]

Over the years, almost without exception, I have noted that Christians, who engage their faith in their workplace, do so because they have a clear understanding of God's presence and purpose regarding their workplace. They see their work as more than a job description that accomplishes the company's goals. They see it as a calling that brings the presence of God into all that their work entails. Grasping this does not necessarily lessen our problems, but it does provide a deep sense of purpose and fulfillment, knowing God can be enjoyed there.

God's Perspective on Work... in His Own Words

In order for us to learn to enjoy God in our work and be a penetrating influence there, we first must shed ourselves of a limited, man-sized view of work. For the Christian, work should mean more than a job description we perform and a paycheck with benefits. Only looking through the lens of God's Word can we properly understand God's definition of work; so let us begin by unpacking the truth in God's Word that defines a God-Sized View of Work.

A Partnership Designed by God

First, we must understand the origin of work. The idea of work did not evolve over time, nor was it created by some ancient industrial genius of the past. The idea of work came directly from God. Work is a reflection of God's character, and a responsibility He has given us. To put it in stronger terms, work is ordained by God and should be viewed as a vocation or calling from God.

In my travels to different parts of the world with FCAP, I met with many different groups of Christians and often asked them to define work. It was not at all unusual to hear someone say that work is like a curse imposed on man by God. Work is neither a curse nor almost one although there are religions and philosophies that have made work out to be that. The Christian world-view is distinctively different. The Bible states that God designed and assigned work for Adam *before* he and Eve fell into sin.[2] In other words, work was not put on humans as a punishment for sin. God's intention for mankind to work came before they rebelled against Him. Though sin affects work, it does not render it useless to God's purposes and His plans.

People have told me that their work seems like a curse or judgment on them because they feel the fatigue of work and see the many problems and difficult people there. Some may ask...Wouldn't you say that is a curse? No, that is not a curse but rather the *effect* of the curse upon work.

We read in Genesis 3:9-19 that when Adam and Eve decided that they did not want to follow God's way the results were catastrophic. God pronounced a curse or judgment upon every aspect of creation because of the rebellion of Adam and Eve. God's verdict, as stated in verse 17-19, directly affects our work.

> Cursed is the ground because of you; In toil you will eat of it all the days of your life. "Both thorns and thistles it shall grow for you; And you will eat the plants of the field; By the sweat of your face you will eat bread, Till you return to the ground, because from it you were taken; For you are dust, and to dust you shall return. (Genesis 3:17-19)

Upon their rejecting God, God placed a judgment on humans that caused them to experience pain and fatigue in their work as well as resistance in their work environment like thorns and thistles. We feel this resistance in many ways today. For example, if your work is serving people, you know all too well that the people you serve can at times irritate and hurt.

Work was designed by God to be a partnership with Him in His creation. God planned for humans to have dominion over His creation.

God blessed them; and God said to them, Be fruitful and multiply, and fill the earth, and subdue it; and rule over the fish of the sea and over the birds of the sky and over every living thing that moves on the earth. (Genesis 1:28)

They were to care for it as a gardener would care for his garden. In her book *Not Just A Job*, Judith Shelly captures in words God's way for our exercising dominion over creation:

Dominion implies control, authority and power. It carries with it great responsibility and ultimate accountability to God. The commission is to care for the earth and its inhabitants with tenderness and love, to rule the world with justice, and to make wise use of the resources He (God) has provided. It is a mandate to share in God's ongoing work of creation.[3]

We are also told "be fruitful and multiply and fill the earth". Our labor has an ability to multiply and provide for people's needs.[4] Again Shelly captures in her book the meaning of this.

God's ongoing work of creation is more than just taking care of what already exists. By commanding Adam and Eve to "be fruitful and multiply" (Genesis1:28), he invited them to join him in creating new life. That command has often been applied exclusively to human procreation... although bearing children is certainly part of the joy in creation that God intends people to share, the context of the passage indicates that there is more to it. In verse 29

God says, "I have given you every plant yielding seed which is upon the face of all the earth." In other words, he has given us the power to reproduce all he has created. He has also given us the satisfaction of seeing the fruit of our labors.[5]

God's design of work has a built-in condition. He allows us to find satisfaction in our work when it is done for reasons bigger than ourselves. What will hinder our view of work from being God-sized is the idea that my work is a God-given responsibility that benefits only me and my family. We must see our work in a greater view, benefitting and impacting others far beyond ourselves and ultimately bringing glory to God.

The Enjoyment of Our Work

Several years ago I worked with a friend of mine named Tom for a few months as I was preparing to finish seminary. Tom's father was a retired Senior Vice President of a leading international corporation. He retired with a sizable income and owned several homes, one in Atlanta, one on the California Coast, and one in Hawaii. At times, when he came to help Tom at his work, he did so because he wanted something to do. Tom informed me that his dad did not know the Lord and that he was discontent and unfulfilled in life. I had some opportunities to talk with Tom's father and something struck me profoundly. Here was a man who had achieved what most men and women were vigorously striving for. Ironically, Tom's dad had gained and achieved everything anybody would ever want but the possessions and fame did not deliver satisfaction or fulfillment. He was no different than those who were still struggling trying to attain such goals.

There is another profound principle for us to grasp in our discovering a God-sized view of work. The enjoyment of work and seeing good from our labor is not based on the amount of our salary or benefits, nor is it found in a company position, or in the amount of vacation time. The enjoyment of our work and seeing good in it comes from the hand of God. One of the wealthiest entrepreneurs of all time understood this all too well. His name was Solomon. He was a king in ancient Israel who pursued and achieved wealth, pleasure, and wisdom to the max. Archeologists are still digging up his treasures. Having achieved all this, listen to his conclusions...they are profound.

> There is nothing better for a man than to eat and drink and tell himself that his labor is good. This also I have seen that it is from the hand of God. (Ecclesiastes 2:24)

> I know that there is nothing better for them than to rejoice and to do good in one's lifetime; moreover, that every man who eats and drinks sees good in all his labor- it is the gift of God. (Ecclesiastes 3:12-13)

> Here is what I have seen to be good and fitting: to eat, to drink and enjoy oneself in all one's labor in which he toils under the sun during the few years of his life which God has given him; for this is his reward. Furthermore, as for every man to whom God has given riches and wealth, He has also empowered him to eat from them and to receive his reward and rejoice in his labor; this is the gift of God. (Ecclesiastes 5:18-19)

If someone tells me something once, he wants me to hear it. If he tells me that same thing twice he wants to emphasize it. Now, if he tells it three times, he really doesn't want me to miss it.

Solomon mentions this not just once, nor twice, but three times in his book of Ecclesiastes. He wants us to get this right...that ultimately the enjoyment of work is not found in things that your company provides but is **"a gift from the hand of God!"** Seeing good in your work is not found in your achievements alone, but that too comes from the hand of God. If work is a "God thing", which it is, and our work is a partnership with Him, then the enjoyment of work cannot be separated from God, the creator and designer of work.

Who Do You Really Work For?

Here again is another one of God's defined principles given to enlarge our view of work beyond the ordinary. People working with a God-sized view of work go to work understanding for whom they work. Christians are instructed to do their work heartily as unto the Lord first of all, rather than unto men and women, because in doing so, we render it a service to Christ.[6] As a Christian, knowing this is absolutely essential for having a healthy attitude in work and being an influence in the workplace.

A few years ago I was asked to attend and speak at one of our local ministry's annual Christmas luncheons where 750 airline people showed up.[7] It was held in a city where a major US airline headquarters was located. When I arrived I was informed that I would be seated at the head table with the airline's CEO and some other top management executives. During the banquet I enjoyed the opportunity of talking with the CEO and one of the Vice Presidents. Though I did not know the CEO's view spiritually, it became apparent to me that he took a real interest in coming to this Christian gathering. I ended my speech with the final words, "I make no apology in telling Christians to do their work first and foremost for Jesus Christ and not their airline. Because when they do, they will be the best asset to their airline." When I returned to my seat, the CEO did not hesitate to respond to my final comments with words I hope to never forget. Leaning toward me he thanked me and told me that he agreed with my comments; that in fact he had seen this attitude in many of the employees present at this banquet, and that was the reason for his coming to the event.

Emphatically the Bible tells us that our work should be done first and foremost as unto to God and not to humans. And it gives some instructions in what this should look like.

> Servants, be obedient to those who are your masters according to the flesh, with fear and trembling, in the sincerity of your heart, as to Christ; not by way of eyeservice, as men-pleasers, but as slaves of Christ, doing the will of God from the heart. With good will render service, as to the Lord, and not to men, knowing that whatever good thing each one does, this he will receive back from the Lord, whether slave or free. (Ephesians 6:5-8)

> Servants, in all things obey those who are your masters on earth, not with external service, as those who merely please men, but with sincerity of heart, fearing the Lord. Whatever you do, do your work heartily, as for the Lord rather than for men; knowing that from the Lord you will receive the reward of the inheritance. It is the Lord Christ whom you serve. (Colossians 3:22-24)

Here are a few observations from these two passages. First of all there are those who would say that these principles apply to slaves, not employees, and therefore do not apply in modern times. However, these verses express not a code of conduct for slaves, but rather timeless truths from our Heavenly Master whom we serve as His servant/slaves. Sadly, we must not forget that the leading occupation of the first century was slavery, of which many were Christians.

As I was teaching a group of airline Christians in Switzerland on the subject of work, I asked them the question, "Why do you think God chose to use in His Scriptures the term servant/slaves instead of employee or professional?" As we discussed this for a moment, a Swissair pilot named Marc said something that struck me. From his perspective he thought God used this term because the use of any other term or position other than "slave" would have ruled out a vast majority of the people in that day, who were slaves. He also said, regardless of our position in our company, we should still consider ourselves as servants of God, who do our work as a service unto Him.

These two passages bring out a few other profound points. One is that our work should be done *"in sincerity of heart."* This means that it is done with an eagerness that comes from within us and is not dependent on outside circumstances. Our motivation should be entirely different from people who don't have a relationship with God. We should not have to wait for the company to give us some kind of bonus or incentive in order to get us to work better or to improve our attitude toward work. Christians have a great opportunity to show the people around them at work who they really work for and why.

We are also told in these passages that we should not be doing our work more enthusiastically when the boss or supervisor is watching us. This kind of work is done for "eye service" or as a "boss pleaser". We are being warned about this because the motivation is wrong. When God is our motivator to do our work our employer never has to worry about keeping an eye on us.

You will not experience true freedom in your work until you understand that doing your work heartily, as to the Lord, is in fact serving Him first. And yes, it will be a service to your company as I told the airline CEO that day. As a Christian you have a different motivation with much greater ramifications. When you seek to achieve excellence in your company job as a service to Christ, you demonstrate to people you are serving One much greater than your company...One who is the Lord of the workplace. In the first few centuries of Christianity, this attitude among Christians transformed the concept of work and challenged the Roman culture of that day. It can transform your workplace today as well!

The Real Reward of Work

There is an ultimate reward for doing our job for God while here on earth. I must tell you, after studying the Bible for years; it was only a few years ago that the reward mentioned in Colossians 3:24 stood out to me as being directly related to your work and workplace. Being familiar with rewards and crowns which Christians will receive in eternity based on their faithful service to God, I wondered why this reward was seldom, if ever taught. Though I figure, it is probably because we lack having a God-sized view of our work.

This particular reward is far more lasting than our wages. It exceeds our benefits and beats any retirement plan. The Colossians 3:22-24 passage tells us that receiving this reward is not based on my company promotions or my exceptional achievements. Rather, my receiving this eternal reward is based on whether or not I did my work enthusiastically as unto the Lord and not just for men.

Most people in your company will work hard with the incentive of money and good work conditions. Some people will even work and strive harder to achieve their career goals and climb the corporate ladder. However, these motives do not stand out in the workplace as something unique or extraordinary. But working with the attitude of doing it wholeheartedly as unto the Lord is not only exceptional - it will catch people's attention. During difficult times when morale is low or attitudes are sour, doing your work as unto the Lord will be glaringly unique.

There is another reward we can gain from our work, while we are still here on earth. It is learning to use our wages and benefits of work as a means to provide for and bless others. We are told that the greater blessing is in giving not receiving.

> You yourselves know that these hands ministered to my *own* needs and to the men who were with me. In everything I showed you that by working hard in this manner you must help the weak and remember the words of the Lord Jesus, that He Himself said, "It is more blessed to give than to receive." (Acts 20:34-35)

We certainly learn this by providing for our family, but it should not stop there. When we have the means, we should learn the blessing of giving to help others in need and supporting ministry in general.[8] If you have not as of yet, start learning now to give some of what you earn so that you can begin to enjoy this reward of work.

Making God Attractive in Our Workplace

In Titus 2:9-10, it goes so far to say that our attitude while on the job and our integrity in our work will be determining factors as to whether or not our belief and faith in God will be attractive to others.

> Urge bondslaves to be subject to their own masters in everything, to be well-pleasing, not argumentative,

not pilfering, but showing all good faith so that they will adorn the doctrine of God our Savior in every respect. (Titus 2:9-10)

Let me focus for a moment on the word "adorn." The word in its original language (Greek) carries the idea of something we all do almost every day. When we get up in the morning and go into the bathroom we "adorn" ourselves; men may shave their face and comb their hair, while ladies may do their hair and put on make-up. All of this is done so that we make ourselves look presentable to those with whom we come in contact. In the same way Christians make their faith in God attractive, when in the details of their work they show integrity, respect, and trustworthiness. How are you adorning your faith in God in the details of your work? Most often it is in the little details of our work that those around us will see the attractiveness of our relationship with God. Certainly the airline CEO who decided to come to the FCAP luncheon saw something attractive about the Christians who worked at his airline.

Being a Christian at my workplace means much more than just working for a pay check to support family and look to experience God's work elsewhere. Going to work as a Christian means doing my job with a God-Sized view of work, where my relationship with God becomes evident in the details of how I do my work and how I treat people. Only then can my work become a service unto Christ and only then will it show as "uniquely Christian"!

DISCUSSION QUESTIONS

1. A coworker comes to you, knowing you're a Christian. He asks how your definition or understanding of work differs from the

company's definition/understanding of work. What would you tell him?

2. The company gives you a job description with responsibilities. How should God's design and purpose of work be affecting the way you carry it out?

3. How would you know whether or not you are doing your job as unto God...or just for the company or for yourself?

4. What are the things at work that hinder me from operating with a God-sized view of work?

5. How does physical and mental fatigue of work affect me and my perception of God's presence, and how do I operate with God's view of work when I am worn out, angry, anxious or fearful?

6. On a scale from 1 to 10 (1- meaning you are working with a Man-sized view of work; and 10- your working with a God-sized view of work), where do you think you are?

2

THE ROOTS OF WORK: PAST AND PRESENT

When I was a teenager, I experienced a great loss in my life. My mother died of cancer. The pain my father, four siblings, and I felt was so very deep. For me her death left a void in my life that only a mother could fill. After a few years, I found myself desiring a deeper relationship with my Grandmother. She had distanced herself from our family after her daughter's death. After some time our relationship became more like a mother-son relationship, even though the miles between us only allowed us to see each other a couple of times a year. I enjoyed this special relationship for 27 years until her death. As I look back, I realize I gleaned more about my roots from the time spent with my grandmother. She openly shared her life, including the good and the bad decisions she had made. Looking back now I realize the effects these decisions had on her, on her two children (my mother and uncle), as well as us, her grandchildren.

All of us come from backgrounds of which the decisions of our ancestors (close and distant ones) have affected us in a number of ways. In a similar way the history of work is like an ancestry. Like family history has affected all of us, so work has changed and been shaped by people throughout history. In order to better understand how work developed to where it is today, we will take a look at its roots and some of its important stages of development in history. This may be quite revealing to you.

In our training I often ask, "Where did the idea of work originate?" Its foundation is laid in the opening pages of the Bible. We see that in the beginning God himself is working. How is he working? He is creating the world and all that is in it, endowing it with order and purpose. Work was not something that God just told us to do; He was doing it Himself. Then God created a special creation in His image and was placed in a special garden. His name was Adam, or man. Why did he do this...for what purpose? We are told in Genesis 2:8,15 that God placed Adam in this garden to cultivate it. The Hebrew word "ābad" used here literally means "to serve". God wanted Adam to know that his work in cultivating the garden was a service to Himself. From this the Jewish people understood work to be ordained of God and a way to serve Him. Another important aspect about work is that God instructed humans to take a rest from work as He did.[1] Resting from our work should not be viewed as somehow unrelated to it but interwoven within God's definition of work.

Work is neither a creation of man nor a creation of your company. It did not in some way evolve out of man's basic need to survive. Work was authorized by God and is an expression of His character and His creation. Why did God give this command to work to our first parents (Adam & Eve) and to us? It is because, as people we bear God's image, and one of the ways we express this image is in our work. In her book *Total Truth*, Nancy Pearcey explains how the image of God connects to work, *"The way we express the image of God is by being creative and building cultures."* [2] God has given us resources in our world whereby we can produce energy that brings efficiency; in the discovering of materials in God's earth we have produced things to build houses, transport people, and cure people. We also have learned how to build educational and medical institutions to help people develop and help those in need. To put it plainly, our work is not a second-class arrangement with God. Pearcey goes on to tell why, *"...Our vocation is not something we do for God - which would put the burden on us to perform and achieve. Instead, it is a way we participate in God's work. For God is engaged not only in the work of salvation but also in the work of preserving and maintaining His creation."* [3] Our working in this world reflects the God who created it and gives us an opportunity to acknowledge His provision for us in our work.

As important as it is for us to understand the origin of work in connection with the Creator and His creation, we must also comprehend the impact the fall of humanity from God had on work. This is essential for our understanding how the view of work has developed up to this point in history.

The Biblical account of "The Fall" (humans rejecting God) tells us what went wrong in the world and its impact on work. The result was chaos and adversity both internally in humans and externally in their environment as a consequence of their rejecting God. The account in Genesis 3 set forth the premise that the world went from a normal state in relation to God and His world to an abnormal one. Because of Adam and Eve's choice to become independent of God and reject His way, the world became abnormal, polluted by selfishness, lust, wrong desire, pride, hatred, fear, and a host of other ills that reside in the heart of humans to this day. The term "The Fall" was coined to identify a past historical event that has continual consequences on humanity and on our work.

People try to explain this abnormality without any reference to God in connection to our environmental or educational problems, thinking that if we could provide better surroundings, more knowledge, and greater resources, we could conquer these problems. Applying this theory to work would mean, if people had better working conditions and newer equipment, they would become more appreciative, and start showing more integrity and respect. Certainly better working conditions and newer equipment can make work easier, but they don't solve the underlying universal problem.

The Biblical explanation describes this abnormality in more personal terms. All of creation, including each individual, is affected by evil and sin. It distorts and corrupts our lives. We see its stain in all of creation. We see and experience its effects daily,[4] as in each of us the principle of sin exists.[5] Sin is said to distort our view and even deceive us from perceiving what is wholesome and right.

You may be thinking... this is somewhat exaggerated or farfetched and does not relate to work or workplace. However, just consider for a moment the costly measures employers have to take in order to insure employees are doing their jobs correctly and efficiently. Companies have created sophisticated computer systems, programs, and even departments to insure employees are working the required time and doing their work completely without cheating the company in some way. Just consider why companies inventory their equipment and materials used on the job. Of course they need to record and stock things, but on the rise are hard facts that show employees are stealing from their companies. Then consider how companies have created Human Resource departments to deal with employee relationships within the workplace.

There is a rather revealing diagnosis of the human condition, described in the book of James.

> What is the source of quarrels and conflicts among you?" (James asks) "Is not the source due to the desires that battle and wage war within you? You lust and do not have; so you commit murder. You are

envious and cannot obtain; so you fight and quarrel. (James 4:1-2)

Sadly, this epitomizes the fallen state of humanity. We can see this played out between two children fighting on a playground, or a conflict between two employees at work, even between two nations at war with one another. All this comes from within the human heart as a result of rejecting God. Under this fallen condition there is inequity of all kinds. As a result, people learn unhealthy tactics in controlling, manipulating, and coercing other people and circumstances. Left unchecked, sin can eventually destroy others as well as our self. One needs not look far to see how these conditions are apparent and affect work and the workplace. We must begin by taking a hard look at ourselves, because sin affects all of us.

History shows that whenever humans disregard God and His design of things, they become tainted with scores of problems. With regard to work, as bad as this may be, the Creation mandate to work has not been entirely lost or destroyed. Pearcey explains, *"The Fall did not destroy our original calling, but only made it more difficult. Our work is marked by sorrow and hard labor."*[6] Having considered how the fallen state of humanity has affected each of us and our work, now let us consider how the idea of work was shaped and reshaped by humans in history.

The Jewish culture, in the Old Testament times, viewed work as an essential part of life. *"The Jews had a saying that he who does not teach his son a trade teaches him to steal."*[7] Here work was thought to be a responsibility of their culture and learned through the family unit. For a person to make the choice not to work, when they were able to, was thought to tempt him or her to steal in order to get the necessities to live. These people saw the importance of encouraging work by providing a good example in their work.

Then came the reign of Ancient Greece and the Greek culture, under which work saw significant changes. The purpose and significance of work began to be reshaped by prominent Greek thinkers like Aristotle, Plato, and Homer. Aristotle told how "*in Thebes no man could become a citizen until ten years after he had stopped working at a trade.*"[8] Obviously working in a trade was not good enough to be a citizen in that culture. Homer even argued that the gods hated mankind and out of spite condemned men to toil or work. Basically, the known world of that day was being told that most work was a curse imposed on humanity by the gods.

Colson and Eckert explain in their book how Plato and Aristotle tried to modify this idea somewhat by offering a two-story concept of work. "*The majority of men should do heavy work so that the minority, like themselves, might engage in higher pursuits, such as art, philosophy, and politics.*"[9] What is conclusive about the Greek culture is that "*artisans and craftsmen were regarded as little better than slaves, while slavery itself was an institution based on a loathing of work.*"[10]

It didn't stop there; the Greek culture's view of work went on to influence the Roman Empire. In his book on how Christianity transformed civilization, Alvin Schmidt explains how the Roman culture viewed work. "*Among the Romans, Cicero (first Century B.C.) said that working daily for a livelihood was unbecoming to a gentleman (freeborn man), and that vulgar are the means of livelihood of all hired workman, whom we pay for mere manual labor...*"[11] Sadly, this view, which belittled work and workers, shaped the culture of that day as well. So much so, that by the time of the end of Caesar Augustus' reign the Roman Empire was made up of approximately one third free men and two thirds slaves.

Then there arose a great light in history, one that

challenged the culture's dominant influence on work and which would eventually reshape it. In a small, remote place there came on the scene of history a person who was a carpenter in Nazareth. His name was Jesus. He claimed to be the Son of God and yet he worked with his hands as a carpenter. Some of the first ones to follow him were mere fishermen from the Sea of Galilee. This profile did not fit into the dominant idea of that day. In the Greek and Roman mindset, if Jesus were that important he would not be doing menial work or working with his hands. According to their perception Jesus should have been talking about people serving Him, rather than Him serving people.[12] To top it off, most of His followers were common workers, tradesmen, and fishermen.

Something else, very interesting, took place the day Jesus started his public ministry. It is one of the few times we read in the Bible about God talking in an audible voice for others to hear. It happened when Jesus had gone to the Jordan River to be baptized. At the baptism, we are told that His Heavenly Father expressed His pleasure in His son, with a voice from heaven, saying, *"You are my beloved son, in you I am well pleased"* (Mark 1:11). Up until this time Jesus had only worked as a common carpenter and had not yet begun His public ministry on earth. In the original text the tense in the wording brings out the idea that His Father was well pleased with all that Jesus had done so far,[13] which was work with His hands as a carpenter. Certainly God the Father was always pleased with His son because of their eternal co-equal relationship. However, here He expresses His delight in His Son working as an "employee" and made a point to connect this as part of His mission while on earth. When I initially heard this I realized the importance of my Lord's example in regard to work.[14]

Without a doubt, Christ and his followers held a radical view about work in comparison to the culture of their day.

"Christianity's beliefs and practices often clashed with the pagan value of the Greco-Roman culture. The Christian view of labor or work as honorable and pleasing was another of the value clashes."[15] The dignity given to the details of work not only clashed with the culture, it undermined slavery, which the culture had created from its distorted view of work.[16] This belief and way of life was liberating to a majority of Christians in the first century AD of whom many were slaves. It is important to understand that the first century church had its birth in an anti-work culture, where free people sought personal pleasure above all else. However, one of the church's greatest impacts on culture was how Christians viewed and performed their work.

The role model of Jesus, His apostles, and His followers was the pattern for the first century church. Christians saw work as an integral part of their spiritual life, and so much so that they encouraged hard work and they abhorred laziness. The Apostle Paul even gave a charge to some Christians in Thessalonica about work. *"If anyone is not willing to work, then he is not to eat, either."*[17] There is more we could divulge, but let's move into an era when the church started having a negative effect on the Biblical idea of work.

By the third century following the resurrection of Christ, Christianity was declared a legal religion of Rome by the Emperor Constantine. Subsequently the church gained more political power and influence within culture and developed into a powerful institution. As this took place, new ideas about work in the world and work in the church were developing. It seemed the church began categorizing work while at the same time dividing its value, somewhat like the Greek's two-story model of work with its greater and lesser value of work. So the church created its own two-story system about work with a different twist. They gave greater value to work in the church and lesser value to all other work apart from the church. This perception of work brought more confusion and contradiction to what had been handed down to them from first century Christians. As they reshaped their view of work came the impression, that people in religious work were doing the "spiritual work" which they esteemed to be more favorable to God. While on the other hand, work done apart from the church was less important to God and was not considered spiritual. The effects of this are still with us today.

This view continued to grow, apparently unchecked, for over a millennium. Its distortion grew in proportion to how much the leadership of the church embraced it. Thankfully, men like Martin Luther and William Tyndale finally came forward to challenge the church's view regarding work. Luther saw that no distinction should be made between the job of a priest/pastor and that of a farmer. He commented, "*The work of monks and priests in God's sight are in no way whatsoever superior to the works of a farmer laboring in a field or a woman looking after her home.*"[18] Then it was the English Reformer, William Tyndale, who said, "*If we look externally, there is a difference between the washing of dishes and preaching of God's word; but as to what pleases God in relation to His call, there is no difference at all.*"[19] These men, and others like them, saw clearly the unbiblical and enslaving dualism that devalued work in their day. For them being a full- time worker for God had little to do with whether or not you worked in the church. God has not assigned greater importance to "spiritual" work and lesser importance to "secular" work. They considered all of it as important to God and understood that "*whatever you do, do all to the glory of God,*"[20] as a full- time service to Him, not part-time. They spoke clearly to their generation, and I think their words need to be heard in our generation as well. Personally, I believe this split view of work is still with us today and many Christians live and work under its enslavement. You may think that I am exaggerating my point. If so, perhaps you should try asking some Christians who work "secular" jobs, this question: "Do you think your work is as important to God and His purposes as the work your pastor is doing in your church or a missionary in a foreign country?" What do you think most would say?

From here we briefly move to the late eighteenth and early nineteenth century. At that time work became known as an Industrial Revolution that gave rise to slavery, child labor, workhouses, and debtor's prison. Great importance was placed on mass production but at the expense of abusing workers. Thankfully, again there were men like Wilberforce and Lord Shaftsbury who *"launched a wave of reforms in the workplace"*[21] in order to abolish this view of slave work and help bring people back to a healthy understanding of work.

In today's world the idea of work is faced with a new set of challenges. With the advancement in computer technology, business has become more of a market driven environment. People's work is not as important as what the stock market forecast looks like on Wall Street. The company's interest is more favorable to the investors than the employee. People who have worked for a company for most of their lives are no longer viewed as an asset but as a liability. Nowadays, with the downturn of the global economy, management, in order to survive, has to make difficult decisions which affect everyone. This creates great stress, distrust, and disillusionment within the relationship of management and employee. The instability of work makes people feel lost at work. Their workplace environment has become more of a survival contest than a job. People are quick to blame corporate greed. Though much of this has been driven by people in high positions who use work for personal gain and control, the struggle with greed is both an employer and employee problem.

Having considered some of the changes work has undergone over the centuries, we must return to its original blueprint. Work was designed by God for humans to exercise their dominion over creation, and built into this design was a relationship that supported the purpose of work. God did not just give Adam work to do; but rather, the relationship they had was tied into the purpose of work. When people feel connected to their work, it's often because their boss relates to them through communication, which reflects appreciation and mutual respect. When this relationship between worker and employer is diminished or dissolved, work becomes distorted and changes. To sum it up, the fallen state of humanity has affected work, and history shows us how this has impacted work and workers.

When Christians uphold their relationship to God at their workplace, they will bring another dimension into it. A Christian cannot underestimate the impact he will make on his work environment and his coworkers. If company conditions deteriorate despite the Christian employee's contributions, the Christian's relationship with God will not be affected. Actually, it is in such times that we become more acutely aware of God's presence, and when we respond to these conditions with His wisdom and guidance, we will be a bright light and positive influence at the workplace.

DISCUSSION QUESTIONS

1. Name some attitudes about work that were portrayed in your home when you were growing up.
2. Why would it be important for us to understand how work is an expression of our being in the image of God?
3. Name some ways you see how "The Fall" of humanity from God affects work today?

4. How did Jesus' occupation as a carpenter and his association with other workers clash with the Greek/Roman culture of that day? Do you believe this part of His early life is understood in today's church?

5. If it was said of Christians in the first few centuries after Christ that their view of work clashed with the culture of that day, how would you say Christians' view of work is clashing with today's work culture? Name some wrong ways in which we could clash with today's work culture. Name some right ways we naturally clash with it.

6. How has the division between secular work versus spiritual work affected you personally? How do you think it affects Christians?

3

EXPECTATIONS
INFLUENCE WORK

The flight was at cruising altitude, when the flight attendant knocked on the cockpit door to ask the pilots if they would like something to drink. The captain took this opportunity to ask her how things were going in the back. Flustered and frustrated she told him what an awful day she was having. She was experiencing some problems with the crew and some difficult passengers. Added to that, she had not expected to have her monthly flying schedule rearranged by the airline. She then expressed that she had not anticipated these problems. The captain, seeing her bewilderment, gently asked: "Do you come to work not expecting to have any problems?" He went on to say: "If so, you are setting yourself up for disappointment and failure every time you come to work."

There are many people, including Christians, who go to work every day with certain expectations about their workplace. Expectations are how we think in the present about what we anticipate in the future. Sometimes expectations arise from promises that were made to us. We also create them when we want to gain or achieve something, or when we become preoccupied with fear or concerns about the future. Some people may tell us we should have no expectations at all. I think that is unrealistic and it is certainly not Biblical. God made us to anticipate things. We offer prayers, expecting things to happen or matters to change. Expectations are not wrong! However, they can cause stress and create false hopes if based on wrong thinking. The flight attendant who felt overwhelmed by her circumstances is an example of how wrong expectations or lack of proper ones caused her to be ill prepared. If she had come to work basing her expectations on a more realistic view of her job, she would have been better prepared to face very common problems in her profession. It is not that we should go to work scouting out problems or be obsessed with them, but neither should we go to work expecting to have no problems at all.

So far we have defined God's purpose of work, and we have also talked about how work has been changed and reshaped over time. Now, we will consider how some common ideas and expectations about work can hinder us from having a God-sized view of work.

Work - An Obsession with Success

We regularly hear stories about people who have achieved what seems like the ultimate goal in life. Either they have reached financial independence or have attained prominent status. Without a doubt, success is most often measured in monetary wealth. Undeniably finances are needed for companies to grow and succeed as well as to provide for people's salaries and benefits. The Christian view about possessions and money does not view them as evil, but puts them in the right perspective. The Bible gives a direct warning, telling us that the love of money and the driving desire to achieve success can become the source of all kinds of troubles.[1] Our work will also be affected in negative ways when it is driven by such ambitions.

We are being bombarded daily with ideas and information that rouse our expectations for greater gain and leads us to believe that success in life is measured by the amount of wages we earn and the things we possess. This is most tempting for people who love competition and thrive on the thrill of risk and results at work. Such a life can be costly, affecting other areas of life. Often family relationships are neglected and friendships are used for personal gain.

Some years ago, when I worked out in a gym on a regular basis, I became friends with a struggling businessman. As a Christian, he wanted so much for God to let him make a million dollars so he could have a greater impact and be a better witness for the Lord. I could see how this desire was having a negative effect on his work and family life. Over a period of time we talked about this, and one day I asked him if he thought God really needed more millionaires to accomplish His purposes in this world. I encouraged him to consider the great impact we can have, regardless of our economic condition, by simply offering our lives to Him, serving Him and others.

Sadly, even among the Christian community much of what has been written on the subject of work gives greater attention to being successful in work through financial gain and status. Christian entrepreneurs can tell their stories of making millions and gaining greater status, but how does that encourage the "normal", hard-working Christian in his workplace? It feeds their imagination and stirs up expectations that life would be better if God would give them success in a better paying job or position. Also, companies looking to hire new employees use enticing tactics to lure people into a job by promising financial and promotional success while little attention is brought to the value of work and its enjoyment. Solomon was a man who accomplished all his goals and achieved more than anyone in his time. He wrote three books in the Old Testament of the Bible. His last book, written probably in his later years, makes statements about life and work that often stagger the mind of its reader. In his book of Ecclesiastes, there is a sobering reminder of how the pursuit of success and striving for great gain can ravage a life and distort work.

In Ecclesiastes, Solomon warns that there are some people who are given great wealth by God and so much so that they lack nothing, but he also tells that what they do lack is the ability to enjoy what they've gained.

> There is an evil which I have seen under the sun and it is prevalent among men-- a man to whom God has given riches and wealth and honor so that his soul lacks nothing of all that he desires; yet God has not empowered him to eat from them, for a foreigner enjoys them. This is vanity and a severe affliction. (Ecclesiastes 6:1-2)

In Ecclesiastes 5:10-11, Solomon also tells us that those who covet money will never be satisfied by it. Why? Because it brings with it a greater capacity for consumption which in turn creates a desire for more. He then draws some interesting contrasts. First, he tells how a laborer will rest pleasantly whether he eats little or much; however, the full stomach of the wealthy won't allow him or her to rest.[2] Then he goes on to say it is much better to be content with one handful (have lesser or little) and enjoy tranquility than to have two hands full (have abundance) and become anxious and restless.[3]

The same magazines and newspapers that report the success stories of rich and passionate business men and women are equally full of stories about these same people whose marriages have failed, whose families have been ruined, or whose careers have ended in corruption and despair. It would do us well to stop and ask ourselves, "Is it the desire for success and gain that motivates me to work?" Such a driving desire can wreck a life!

Success cannot empower you to enjoy what it promises to give you. You may gain things and achieve status at work, but without God's gracious hand you cannot enjoy anything. Solomon tells us again, that the greatest result that comes from a man or woman's labor is not money, benefits, or position; it simply and profoundly is the ability to enjoy the results, whether little or much, of his or her labor.[4]

Though God has not allowed everyone to be rich with material things, He has given every one of His children a spiritual inheritance that provides a quality of life, not derived from the things themselves. This quality is offered to both those who are not rich and to those who are. It consists of God occupying their life with gladness of heart with whatever little or much they have.[5] Do you have this quality of life, or are the things you strive for at work weighing you down? Jesus told his disciples that possessing and enjoying life is not found in being occupied in the pursuit of such things. Why? Because the real quality of life comes from seeking God first and submitting to His rule in our life and in our work. Then all the other things can be enjoyed.[6] Let's move on to another faulty way of thinking that could keep us from having a God-sized view of work.

The Key to My Happiness and Security

A good friend of mine told me that when his airline company hired him over 20 years ago, it was doing so well that they unofficially told the new hires to go out and buy a house and car because they would be taken care of the rest of their lives.

In my years in FCAP I have seen a peculiar tendency among Christians regarding the success or failure of their company. When things are going well, profits are high, bonuses are forthcoming, and the company is expanding, some Christians tend to start spiritualizing their company. They can do this in different ways; first, by explaining that their company's prosperity is because it was founded on spiritual principles which brought God's hand of blessing on it. Then I've heard other people explain their company's success was because of its good Christian leadership. Is this so? In some cases I know, for a fact, it is. Also, I am convinced that when management and employees of any company follow God's principles in their work, it will bring results which honor God.[7]

However, my concern is not so much how Christians interpret their company's success. It's what happens once they've convinced themselves that their company is now their security because God is blessing it. They can subtly be tempted to put their trust in their company for their future wellbeing. Such misguided views about your company won't last in an ever-changing world!

Suddenly the company which you've given your allegiance to is faced with huge financial challenges, for reasons you may or may not be aware of. With notices of cutbacks and layoffs, people's attitude can change drastically about their trusted company. The sense arises that their trust has been betrayed, and their emotions now shift from relying on their company to becoming discontent, even to the point of blaming and slandering their employer. The problem intensifies especially when companies break promises without giving reasons or explanations. The relationship between employer and employee is broken because of misplaced trust.

We must not forget that the Sovereign Lord, who is unchangeable in His character, is our great provider and guide. He said, *"I will never leave you nor forsake you."*[8] Even when facing pay cuts or layoffs, He has promised to provide for our needs.

It was the prophet Jeremiah who divided mankind into two groups of people in chapter 17 of his book...*those who trust in the Lord and those who turn away from the Lord and put their reliance on human strength.* Israel had a history of depending on Egypt and other nations for provision and protection in times of crisis, instead of relying on the Lord. Jeremiah foretold how people whose trust is in the Lord would be blessed. *"For he will be like a tree planted by the water, that extends its roots by a stream and will not fear when the heat comes; But its leaves will be green, and it will not be anxious in a year of drought nor cease to yield fruit.."*[9] But he also warns of the consequence for those who turn away from trusting God, *"For he will be like a bush in the desert and will not see when prosperity comes, but will live in stony wastes in the wilderness, a land of salt without inhabitant."*[10]

Am I suggesting that you should live with the expectation that your company will fail? No, not at all! My intent here is not to paint a gloom and doom picture of your company, but rather a realistic one. If your company is strong and doing well, thank God for it and show your appreciation of it! But, if your company is facing turbulent and hard times, your responsibility is to pray for it and continue doing your work heartily as unto the Lord.

Some of you may be feeling the sting and sadness of having gone through such a collapse in a former company. May I encourage you not to let the memory of such dashed expectations turn into bitterness and resentment, but continue to look to God for His provisions and guidance.

Let's look at one more...

Motivated By Favorable Conditions

There is much that could be said about a company's work environment. Certainly it is not only important... it is the right thing for companies to provide a good work environment and give their employees a healthy motivation in doing their work. Incentives, like extra pay for extra time, or bonuses for exceptional work, are not only good ways to reward hard work, but they also demonstrate that the company recognizes and appreciates the employee's contribution in making it what it is.

However, the reality in today's work environment is that the employee's work time is being compressed by reducing the workforce and increasing responsibilities. Recently a lady told me that the training department of her company used to employ four people. However, facing the economic realities her company had to downsize, and she now is the only employee left in her department. Needless to say, she felt overwhelmed with all the work. Company management and leaders need to give greater attention to these challenges. Just cutting positions and adding more responsibility is not always the answer. This can bring fear and anxiety into the workplace, which can discourage employees and affect the overall outcome of the company.

It is gratifying to work for a company that encourages a healthy work environment. A place where leadership sets the example even if it means they are the first to take pay cuts. Company leadership that sets its own example of fairness and sacrifice makes such a greater impact on the employees than the typical pep talks that are often given to cover up the real issues.[11]

But what if you are working for a company with a dysfunctional work environment? How can one be motivated in such conditions? Do you just grit your teeth, try to get the job done to survive, and that's it?[12]

In the first few centuries after the resurrection of Christ, the early Christians (many of whom were slaves) were energized in their work with a motivation greater than what their master or repressive culture provided. The Christian faith in the first few centuries thrived in the workplace because Christians brought something greater into it.[13]

What compelled them to exceed under the pressures of

their work environment? It was the power of God's love that influenced their lives in a greater way than anything else in the culture. The Apostle Paul speaks about the love of Christ as a constraining yet compelling force in those who trust God.[14] The New Bible Commentary sheds light on this: *"Christ's love aroused the love and awe for God which produced his (Paul's) 'insane' enthusiasm. The word in the original for **constrain** implies that it forcibly compresses all energies into one effort or path."* [15] Experiencing God's love comes as you receive Him in life's circumstances, like at work. When we know this truth in our workplace, as the first century Christian slaves did then, it will become a greater compelling force than anything else around us.

The early Christians who were slaves understood this. They saw themselves as more than personal property of a human master. They identified themselves as slaves of Christ who were bought and loved by Him. They did their work to and for the glory of God. They did not need to be coerced nor threatened to do their work. They simply did it from a heart of gratitude, knowing their Master, Jesus Christ, who loved them and would reward them for such a service.[16] However tough their work environment may have been, they were told not to seek retribution or pay back wrong with wrong. They knew that their master on earth must give an account to God someday as to how they treated their servants and workers.

> And masters, do the same things to them, and give up threatening, knowing that both their Master and yours is in heaven, and there is no partiality with Him. (Ephesians 6:9)
>
> Masters, grant to your slaves justice and fairness, knowing that you too have a Master in heaven. (Colossians 4:1)

For the Christian to go to work with any less of a motivation is a travesty. When I expect my company or union to provide an environment for me to be motivated to do my job diligently, then my Christian faith makes no difference at the workplace. Jesus illustrated how we are to be people of distinct influence. He told his followers that when a soldier asks you to carry his helmet one mile (which they could do under Roman law), then you should be willing to go the extra mile and carry it two miles instead of one.[17] Jesus knew that for a Roman soldier to see a Christian do this meant they were being motivated by something greater than Roman law. This kind of motivation was unheard of in Roman culture, which was debase and self-serving. Their law was biased and benefitted only their own. There is no greater motivation than doing your work unto God...anything less will diminish your distinctiveness there.

A few years ago my wife and I were in Europe for meetings with some FCAP groups. We were traveling on a Swiss train from Zurich to Bern. As the refreshment cart came down the aisle, I couldn't help but notice the young man managing it. He had a pleasant and joyful expression on his face and was treating the passengers with great kindness and consideration. My wife, being Swiss, noticed that after the young man would finish serving a customer, he would end by saying, "May God bless you!" in Swiss. Though this is a very common thing to say in America, it is not common in Switzerland. Actually, it can be unusual and unexpected, especially when someone says this to a stranger in public. While he was serving our coffees, we had an opportunity to talk with him. He told us his name was Hans, and we soon found out that he was a Christian. But what was more encouraging and refreshing was his comment about his job. I had mentioned to him how we enjoyed watching him do his work cheerfully and graciously. He answered by saying: "I see my work as a service to God and a ministry to these people. As I am planning to go to another country as a missionary, I realized that if I cannot show the love and mercy of God to my own people in my everyday workplace, then I am not fit to be a missionary elsewhere. That is why I got this job." Obviously Hans' motivation for doing his work was much greater than having a comfortable job in the stable environment of a Swiss company. Hans brought a spiritual dimension into an oblivious work environment and influenced it for God's glory!

Why not take some time to consider some of the beliefs and expectations you hold about your work and your company. Ask God to examine your heart to reveal any misplaced trust or unrealistic expectations you may have. Then ask Him to transform your view of work into His God-sized one!

Discussion Questions

1. As you were looking for a job, what expectation did you have of it?
2. When you got your job, how was it different from the expectations you had?
3. What are some personal expectations you have from work on a daily basis?
4. In this chapter we discussed three faulty expectations that will influence work. Name some additional faulty expectations about work that could hinder a Christian from being a spiritual influence.
5. Describe what happens when we go to work putting our trust in the company instead of God.
6. What truths from God's Word do I need to bring to work that can prevent me from falling into the trap of faulty expectations?

SECTION 2

DEFINING
WORKPLACE
MINISTRY

WHEN
GOD
SHOWS UP AT
WORK

4

WORKPLACE MINISTRY... WHAT IS IT?

May I ask you to ponder upon the following. The word "ministry" can raise a multitude of perceptions, classifications, and expectations. What comes to mind when you hear the word "ministry"? You might say that ministry is about people connected to a church who meet in a building, or that ministry is the work of a person dressed in distinctive clothes who has a title in front of his or her name. Some of you might respond to ministry in terms of programs and events which a church may provide, such as Sunday morning worship and preaching services, or children, youth, college and career programs. Now, let me expand the question by asking, "What do you think when you hear the word "ministry" in connection to or with the workplace?" What do you think your coworkers' responses would be if they heard you talk about ministry in the workplace? Maybe some would assume you are advocating the use of company time to proselytize and preach on the job. Undeniably, the word "ministry" in connection with the workplace could raise a lot of questions from people, both inside and outside of the Christian faith. In this chapter we will define ministry and consider the relationship it has to our work and workplace.

Shortly after becoming director of FCAP, I started meeting for in-depth discipleship with a couple of young men who work in the airline industry. I found great joy in doing this over the years, and these guys have become best friends of mine. At one of our meetings, early on, Scott asked if he could talk with me afterward, mentioning he had some exciting news. I speculated that it may be about a promotion, or perhaps he was being transferred or given a bonus. I was eager to hear his news, so we went into my office to talk privately. He looked at me intently saying: "Paul, I think God wants me to quit my job and go into the ministry!" I must have looked a bit stunned because his expression went from being poised to puzzled. My first thought was…where did this idea come from? But quickly I decided I should find out more, so I asked him what had prompted him to consider this path. His answer was not a complete surprise to me. He said he felt God could use him in a greater way in the ministry field than in his present job. The way things worked out, Scott stayed in his airline job, and within a few years I watched how his outlook changed. As we talked and prayed about ministry, he began to see things differently about his job and ministry opportunities there. Soon after this he told us, "I realize now I am in the ministry and go to it every time I enter my workplace." Since then, it has been a privilege for me to see both of these men grow spiritually and to witness how their ministries have developed and multiplied in the workplace. They are true examples of how ministry takes place in the workplace.

What changed Scott's thinking from the idea that he needed to leave his job to go into the ministry to the idea that going to work meant entering the ministry? Over the years on a number of occasions, I have heard people share with me that they wanted to quit their jobs and go into full-time ministry. Some have done so for the right reasons, and others have done this because, like Scott, they thought work in the church had a much higher calling and offered greater ministry opportunities than working a "regular" job. What I discovered from my conversations with people over the years is that there are at least five different ways Christians understand ministry in relation or connection to their work and workplace.

Common Ideas about Ministry in Relation to Work

Some Christians understand work's relationship to ministry to mean that work is a way to provide wages so that funds can be used to support ministries like churches, missions, or special projects outside of the workplace. This idea about ministry and work does not see ministry as woven into work but sees ministry only as a beneficiary of work.

There are other Christians who see ministry in relationship to their work to mean that they should bring their local church programs and methods into their workplace to reach people. Others may see their work environment as a place to incorporate evangelism strategies, handing out their local church's brochure or special tracts. I know of some Christians who gather people together during their break time at work to show a DVD of their church's Sunday message. These attempts are not wrong but may represent a limited view of ministry.

Then there are Christians who think they have to wait or seek out an obvious Divine intervention or a Divine activity to spontaneously pop up for ministry to take place. One must look for and discover it in order to get involved. They may be hoping to cross paths with someone who is obviously looking for God, or maybe they are watching for an opportunity to minister in an event which seems to have God's fingerprints on it. Certainly God can and does work in such ways. However, I believe this view minimizes the capacity of ministry for a Christian in his workplace. We must consider this important truth...God has put His treasure in each of us[1] in order to bring about ministry through us in every circumstance of life.

Then again there are some Christians who believe ministry does not relate to work at all; that the two are incompatible and should not be carried out simultaneously. They view the two as separate compartments of life; one as their spiritual arena where ministry takes place, and the other as their secular area wherein one works a job. Interestingly, this view seems to indicate that the Christian life is more like a leisure activity rather than it encompassing all of life.

Lastly, there are those who see ministry as an integrated and influential part of their work. They understand that workplace ministry does not operate in the same way as in their local church but see it as a fulfilling and complimenting part of the church's mission. The remainder of the book will explain and illustrate this view of ministry and work.

Who is in The Ministry?

Our understanding of ministry needs to take into consideration its broad Biblical definition and the description of how it should function. We also need to consider its relationship to our work and workplace.

First, let us consider what is required to be involved in ministry. A Biblical view of ministry does not confine it to parameters of the local church or to be solely practiced by certain designated people. Such a view diminishes the vast possibilities for the Christian's involvement in ministry. For instance, when a church infers that full participation in their ministry requires a seminary degree, an ordination process, or a special calling, it fosters a limited view of ministry. Certainly, there is nothing wrong with people earning seminary degrees or obtaining qualifications through ordination processes. Such requirements are often applied to those pursuing vocational ministry.

God has designed certain positions within the church that

are to be filled by people whose lives are exemplary of the faith and who aspire to serve by carrying out particular responsibilities. There are examples of this in the Old Testament. The titles of Priest and Prophet were given to certain people who carried out God-given responsibilities. In the Old Testament the prophets were responsible to speak on behalf of God to proclaim His message in order to call people back to God. The priests were to carry out the practical functions in the tabernacle and temple. In the New Testament, titles such as Apostle, Prophet, Elder, and Deacon were also given which described particular positions tied to practical responsibilities. For example, the apostles were eyewitnesses of Christ sent out to establish people in the truth of the Gospel message. Elders were spiritual shepherds over a local group of people and were to lead by their example. These positions were not thought to be all encompassing of ministry. Instead they represented God-given responsibilities which were a functional part of God's total ministry. The First Century believers did not isolate ministry to a certain class of people within the church. They saw ministry as the responsibility of all Christians, not just a selective group.

In 2 Corinthians chapters 3 and 4, the Apostle Paul drew a comparison between the Old and New Covenant Ministry. In the Old, God chose to show His glory through certain people and places in special ways. However, under the New Covenant, God has chosen to abide in His people and work through them in their everyday settings of life.

> But whenever a person turns to the Lord, the veil is taken away. Now the Lord is the Spirit, and where the Spirit of the Lord is, there is liberty. But we all, with unveiled face, beholding as in a mirror the glory of the Lord, are being transformed into the same image from glory to glory, just as from the

Lord, the Spirit. (2 Corinthians 3:16-18)

All who turn to the Lord are said to behold His glory. As we behold Him two things happen; He begins to transform us into His image and we begin to reflect His glory to those around us.

Most scholars believe there should not have been a chapter division placed between verses 3:18 and 4:1 because it is here that Paul explains who and how people qualify to minister under the New Covenant. In verse 4:1 we read, "*Since* **we** *have this ministry...*" Who is meant by "**we**"? According to verse 16, it is everyone who has turned to the Lord. Involvement in new covenant ministry is inclusive of all Christians.

There are several reasons why Christians have felt restricted from seeing themselves as being fully involved in ministry. Over the centuries the church has established certain terms that classify Christians in regard to whether or not they are involved in church ministry. These are not found in the Bible, yet they have been ingrained in the church. The two most common terms we have heard are "Clergy" and "Laity."[2] In the minds of most people, clergy describes a Christian who either received special training or has some kind of higher calling in order to be qualified for ministry. While the term laity is used to describe ordinary people who have no special calling or professional training. People's perception from this is that the laity are those who support, follow, and attend the activities of the clergy, which to some point is accurate. We do follow and support those who lead us according to God and His Word. But this can be misunderstood if we don't see that the "clergy's" responsibility is to equip the "laity" for their involvement in ministry.

And He gave some as apostles, and some as prophets, and some as evangelists, and some as pastors and teachers, for the equipping of the saints for the work of service, to the building up of the body of Christ. (Ephesians 4:11-12)

Underlying Characteristic

The New Testament gives us a portrait of ministry through our Lord's example of servanthood.[3] Also, within the terms used to describe and define ministry in the New Testament this servant living is underscored. In the English Bible the words *ministry, minister,* and *ministering* are all derived from Greek words that carry the same root idea that focus on this underlying truth. The word *doulos* translated means "slave" or "servant". Another common Greek word of that day was *diakonein,* describing how ministry was compared to performing a menial service like a table waiter who served people. Then there was the word *douleuein,* which put emphasis on the lordship and ownership of a servant/slave. These words for the most part have been translated in one form or another with the word ministry or service. Ministry was characterized as a service to others, done by those who saw themselves as slaves or servants of Christ. The church in the first century clearly understood that whether you were an apostle, prophet, teacher, elder, deacon, or just a "normal" person, all service rendered was done as a slave or servant of Christ... whether you washed the feet of your houseguests, prepared meals, or preached the Word of God.

Listen to how Peter, Paul, James and Jude, Apostles and eyewitnesses of Christ, described their ministry status in their own words. Peter a *bondservant* of Jesus Christ... Paul a *servant* of Christ Jesus... James a *bondservant* of Christ... Jude a *bondservant* of Jesus Christ... They considered themselves *bondservants of Jesus Christ!*[4] They did not see themselves in a special ministry position which elevated them above the status of a servant. Nor did they give themselves any special titles which placed them and their work above that of being a bond slave of Jesus Christ.

> Let a man regard us in this manner, as servants of Christ and stewards of the mysteries of God. (1Corinthians 4:1)

Sadly, in these days, to be in leadership of a ministry is often more about personality and status rather than servanthood. When any ministry elevates itself to titles and positions and disregards service, it is a contradiction to the ministry of our Lord. False elevation communicates to people that their "regular" jobs, like housework, schoolwork, civic responsibilities, etc. are only menial and don't mean as much to God as ministry done by people with a "higher calling". Because of actions like these, the broader meaning of ministry which applies to all Christians has become tainted and imbalanced.

According to Christ, the more our life is characterized as a servant, the better we are qualified for leadership in ministry.

> Calling them to Himself, Jesus said to them, "You know that those who are recognized as rulers of the Gentiles lord it over them; and their great men exercise authority over them. But it is not this way among you, but whoever wishes to become great among you shall be your servant; and whoever wishes to be first among you shall be slave of all. For even the Son of Man did not come to be served, but to serve, and to give His life a ransom for many." (Mark 10:42-45)

There is no greater position in the church of Jesus Christ

than that of being a servant of Jesus Christ, because serving truly reflects our Lord's ministry while He was on earth.

> Have this attitude in yourselves which was also in Christ Jesus, who, although He existed in the form of God, did not regard equality with God a thing to be grasped, but emptied Himself, taking the form of a bond-servant, and being made in the likeness of men. (Philippians 2:5-7)

This overriding attribute of ministry has direct application to our work and workplace. With this understanding, Christians engage in workplace ministry.

Ministry in Relationship to Our Workplace

Building upon this Biblical model for ministry, we recognize that in our jobs we regard ourselves as servants of Christ. Doing our work heartily unto Christ is providing a service (ministry) unto the Lord and not merely to men.[5] Don't miss this! God is saying that as you perform your company's job description this way, you participate with Christ in ministry at your workplace. As a Christian, if you see your work as anything less than this, you will miss the opportunity of workplace ministry!

As previously mentioned, a complete understanding of ministry in relation to work does not divide work and ministry into separate compartments; they do and should overlap. We are whole people! Our faith and obedience to God is to be evident in our total life experience, not just designated parts which we've labeled as "private" and "sacred". Whatever we do...we do all for the glory of God![6] Ministry in the workplace is bringing our relationship with God into the details of work and workplace.

As an employee you have been equipped and trained to

perform your job for your company. However, as a Christian, you have an added dimension you cannot afford to overlook. Your faith in the Lord should be integrated into the details of the job you have been trained to do. If not, then your job could become nothing more than a routine and your faith alienated from your work. God designed our faith in Him to influence our work, giving the routine of our work a deeper purpose and meaning. It brings value to the little things we say and do and a deep realization that something much bigger is being accomplished in it all. Does your job description have this added dimension to it?[7]

Many churches keep records of their members' attendance on Sundays, but God carries out His ministry in our workplaces by His attendance through us there. The essence of workplace ministry is about God declaring His glory through us in our companies as we perform our jobs and serve the people God has placed around us.

Leaving a Legacy in Workplace Ministry

I would like to dedicate the remainder of this chapter to a man whose life left a legacy of ministry in the workplace. His life not only touched many people in his workplace, it personally had an impact on my own life.

I was in my third year with FCAP when we received a call from a man who had started a prayer group in his workplace. He introduced himself as Clarence and told me how the group got started six months earlier. Clarence's group had just heard about FCAP, and he called to let us know that the group wanted to connect with our ministry. Their desire was to identify with other Christians in the industry.

Clarence shared why and how the group had started, "One Sunday morning in April, while at church, I heard the voice of the Lord. I don't think it was an audible voice, but God told me...'Clarence it is time to pray!'" Now, you may be thinking the same thing I did. Pray? When, where, and about what? I am a firm believer in prayer, but my interest was how Clarence related this to his workplace. I had already seen some Christians start up prayer meetings at work, modeled in the fashion of a typical church prayer meeting, praying primarily for matters going on outside of work and their own lives. What I would eventually observe from this dear man's prayer life would serve as a model and example for me and others of effective workplace ministry.

Clarence started his group by inviting Christians he knew around him at work to take 20 minutes out of their lunch break to focus on the Lord and to pray. He had asked the management for a room. At first his request was not granted, as management wasn't sure what Clarence's meeting was all about. So the group decided to meet in an area where new construction was being done on the building. When the construction workers would go on their lunch break, Clarence's little group would find a place amidst all the construction materials to meet. A few months had passed when management approved their meetings and provided them a room.

At the end of my initial phone conversation with Clarence he invited me to join them at one of their meetings. I was to share the ministry of FCAP with the group and to pray with them. I was looking forward to visiting their group as this is something I have loved to do in FCAP over the years - be with people in their workplace!

As I was driving to meet with them for the first time, I honestly was thinking to myself, "Twenty minutes is not a very long time for effective ministry to take place. For most church meetings twenty minutes is hardly enough for a warm-up time." Well, for as long as I live and have a sound mind, the impressions of that meeting will remain with me. That day the

Lord gently let me know that I needed to expand my narrow way of thinking. I was about to learn what kind of ministry can happen in twenty minutes!

Clarence met me at the reception desk at the entrance of his building and took me to their room. Their meeting room was small but nice; it could seat about twenty people comfortably. It was 12:00 noon when we entered the room and no one was there. However, within five minutes the room was packed with around 35-40 people, most of them were standing. It was time to start. There was no big introduction, no song service, no eloquent sermon, nor some supernatural sign to set "the mood". They read a few scriptures and zeroed in on a few truths, nothing vague or general, but precisely addressing the tough challenges and issues of work which these men and women were facing. Then people started sharing prayer requests, not just prayers for themselves or people in distant places, but most of them were for their coworkers and situations at work, as well as some personal ones. I quickly realized this was a unique prayer meeting. These people were passionate about praying for what was happening around them at work. After I briefly shared about the ministry of FCAP and a few thoughts from Scripture, they got right down to praying for the requests. They also prayed for the director of their center who was in charge of over 1,400 people in their building and for the company's upper management and supervisors. They prayed for about ten minutes. Then as quickly as the room had filled up it was vacated and everyone returned to his or her work. When I left the meeting that day, I was thoroughly invigorated by watching these people engaging their faith and connecting through prayer. Their view of ministry in the workplace was dynamic and alive.

Not much later, Clarence called and asked me again to come and visit their group. At the end of their 20-minute meeting, he pulled me aside into a corner of the room to meet with a lady whose husband was leaving her. This lady had come to the meeting because a person from the prayer group, who was working next to her, had become aware of her situation and had reached out to offer help in her crisis. As we were praying with this lady she cried, and we assured her of our love and support. Three weeks later, I received a call from Clarence telling me that the lady had become a Christian.

The ministry dynamics of this group grew and their stories kept rolling in. They believed in working heartily as unto the Lord and in praying for God's presence to bring His influence through them into their workplace. Sometime later, when their airline was merging departments and employees were being relocated, the group saw an open door for new ministry opportunities in a very practical way. They reached out to fellow employees who had to move into the area and in creative ways helped them, even after work. Clarence told me the story of how one of these employees and her whole family wanted to give their lives to Christ because they saw Christ through the love and care they received from the group.

It became more and more obvious to me that the people in this group understood clearly how God desired to uniquely use each of them in their area at work. I came to the realization that their 20-minute meeting was more of a celebration and coordination of what God was doing through each of them throughout the workday. Their presence influenced the whole work operation. So much so, that at times even a few managers came to the group meeting to ask for prayer.

In late January 2011, we received the news that Clarence died suddenly due to health challenges he had been experiencing in recent years. It was a shock to us and especially to the people in the group. My last visit with Clarence and the group was five months before he went to be with the Lord. As usual I had come away filled with joy and appreciation for their reflection of God's work. Leaving him that day, I asked Clarence when he was going to retire (He was in his 60's and had been with the company some 30 years.) He answered me with a smile and somewhat kiddingly, "My wife is asking me the same question." Then with a serious yet humble look he said, "Brother Paul, I don't want to leave one day earlier than God's got for me here because there are still so many ministry opportunities." Clarence's heart beat for the ministry of His Lord for whom he was a diligent, faithful servant.

His airline gave the group a bigger room to hold a service in his memory. They waited a few months to have it, so it would coincide with the 16th anniversary of the group. They announced it as "A Celebration of Clarence's Life - 16 Years of Praying in the Workplace." I had the privilege to speak at that service, but what was more thrilling for me that day, was to hear four people share how God changed their lives radically because of their contact with Clarence and the people in this group. One of them was a girl who shared that she had been a drug addict and alcoholic. Though she was still able to do her work, everyone knew she had a problem. One day Clarence met her during work and simply said, "Sister, God's got a better life for you." In time they not only watched her come to faith in Christ, but they encouraged and helped her through the process of becoming free from her addictions. I would need another chapter in this book to write down all the stories I heard from him and about the group. Their lives are a testimony that God loves to work through us in our workplace, and Clarence's life left a legacy of fruit from His labor.

Why is it that many of us want to look to our churches to provide us with ministry opportunities, when there are so many of them around us at work? This is what workplace ministry is all about. It starts by first having a rendezvous with God in our work, then being aware of the people around us at work, and finally using the circumstances at work. All three are an integral part of our understanding and involvement in workplace ministry... and it is **God's way of showing up at work.**

DISCUSSION QUESTIONS

1. What is the first thing that comes to your mind when you hear the word "ministry?"

2. What comes to your mind when you hear the word ministry used in connection with the workplace?

3. Now, what would you say people's impressions are when they hear you use the word ministry in connection with the workplace?

4. Have any of the points under "Common Ideas about Ministry in Relation to Work" affected your view of ministry at work? How?

5. How can a correct view of ministry help Christians be more of a spiritual influence on the job? How can a limited or incorrect view of ministry hinder this influence?

6. If God's model of leadership has to do primarily with serving, how can we incorporate this while fulfilling our job responsibilities? How can managers, supervisors and owners incorporate God's model of leadership?

5

WORKPLACE MINISTRY... A CHALLENGING ENVIRONMENT

It was early on with FCAP when I received a letter from a lady asking for my advice. She was young and was looking for her first big job in the airline industry. She expressed how she wanted to serve the Lord by becoming a flight attendant. I thought that was great, but what caught my attention were her comments that followed. I quickly gathered that she wanted to work ONLY for a certain kind of company. She explained her search. The first company she mentioned was a major airline; she did not want to work for them because its CEO was known to be immoral. Next, she went on to explain why she would not seek employment with another particular airline because of the potential turbulence between them and a union. Finally, she brought up the name of a third company and shared how she could not approve of that company's diversity policy. Then she asked me the million dollar question, "Would you suggest an airline in which I could best serve the Lord?" I tried to explain that her expectations were not realistic. That is...to find an airline company that would provide the kind of spiritual environment she was seeking. I went on to say that the key is not finding a Christian company to work for but living out her Christian faith in whatever company she chose to work. I certainly would not discourage anyone from seeking employment in a healthy company, as I would want that for myself, but the truth is that even the best ones have their issues and can go through changes. I admire this young lady's desire to serve God at work, but I am concerned for her and others like her who think the potential of their service to God in the workplace is dependent on how well the environment there is suited to their faith. Actually the opposite is true! Christ calls his people out into the world every day as his agents to bring influence and change. The truth is that we often discover in the tough adversities of life, not our potential but God's! Ministry in the workplace offers us the opportunity to better understand and define our faith walk with God. It teaches us how to express God's ministry in unique ways, even in an unwelcoming environment. The workplace is not a place for Christians to have their faith pampered, for even the spiritually fit will feel its challenges.

We will not spend time making a list of the problems in the work environment as usually it is not difficult for employees to list such problems. In general we know it could consist of complaints like greed, unfairness, favoritism, etc. We will look at a few characteristics of which we should be aware in the work environment. Hopefully, by the end of this chapter you will have a better grasp of the work environment to which you have been called to minister.

The Forces at Work

We use the word "workforce" to describe a number of employees working together to carry out a specific activity toward a common goal in the company. Together their cooperative efforts accomplish a bigger purpose. For instance, a flight heading from Atlanta to Munich requires a varied coordination of employees and equipment. This workforce is made up of flight operations, ground people, mechanics, airport/gate agents, baggage handlers, as well as cabin and flight deck crews; all of whom work together to carry out this purpose.

Using this analogy, do you realize that there are other forces constantly at work around you in your workplace? I don't mean the company workforce, but spiritual forces that coordinate their efforts in trying to alter your attitude and actions to conform to a purpose quite contrary to the Christian faith. As we are performing our jobs, we need to be aware that the workplace environment has an assortment of beliefs, morals, and values, capable of clashing with one another.

Here is how it works: whether you realize it or not, there are conditions in your work environment that are pressing you to conform. The Bible gives some details on how this pressure works.

> And you were dead in your trespasses and sins, in which you formerly walked according to the course of this world, according to the prince of the power of the air, of the spirit that is now working in the sons of disobedience. (Ephesians 2:1-2)

Because the world system is set on a course of disregarding God and His ways, we are told a coordinated effort is being promoted by the Evil One - Satan. His goal is to shape an energizing force with a growing number of people. The Bible refers to this as "the spirit that works in them." Here is an example how this can happen in the workplace environment. Something takes place to which people respond or react, like a growing attitude of anger toward the company or certain group of employees. People begin to express their frustration or resentment with words or gestures. As they share their views, they lead others to believe things that may or may not be true. The more people join their attitude, the more the spirit of what they believe intensifies and becomes a dominant trait. As this happens, you will feel it pressuring you to conform to it. Perhaps you could resist from giving in to their ways. But, even if you can, the threat of this pressure could still paralyze you from doing the right thing or expressing it in the right way.[1]

Certain jobs and positions seem to come with built-in bad habits that are kind of like traits of the job. For example it has become the habit of people in certain "higher" positions to subtly put down those in other positions, because it supposedly has always been the tradition and it makes their own position look better. This kind of behavior became more evident to us, when we conducted a think-tank meeting a few years ago with eight in-flight people. Half of them were flight attendants and the other half pilots. I asked them to describe any bad traits that existed between them. They openly talked about how they practiced subtle put downs by joking about each other and how they lacked consideration for one another. To our surprise, we began to realize the negative effect this was having on their work environment and how they had conformed to this as something normal.

We often don't identify something like this immediately. It gradually works itself undetected into us before we become aware of it. I have a good friend who shared with me how she was drawn into such a situation and how she eventually conformed and succumbed. Her airline was going through difficulties, and management was handing down decisions that were obviously in their own interest and not in the interests of the company or the employees. As a Christian she was working with people whose views were quite different from hers. One day at work she found herself in a discussion with a few co-workers who openly expressed their disappointment and resentment toward management. She described how she remained calm outwardly, but inside she began agreeing with them. As the conversations continued, she began following their same train of thought, even to the point of sharing their rationale and resentment. Then she began expressing her agreement vocally with them, which lead her to add a few of her own personal grievances. She told me the more she adapted to their ways, the more she felt energized. Not until she walked away from the conversation, did she realize how she had conformed to their negative spirit at work.

This is how the spiritual workforce of this age works. It draws us into discontentment, complaining, resentment, anger, and a host of other ills at the workplace. Initially it may be only one person who expresses his frustrations, but this kind of attitude can quickly escalate as others join in. Your work environment can be likened to a battleground. The Bible depicts this, not as a battle against people or the company, but as a spiritual one that is being waged in its own way. If we are not careful, we will fall into its scheme by utilizing the same worldly tactics which are used against us. This will have altering negative effects on our attitude toward the people around us and on our work performance.

Our spiritual effectiveness in the workplace means being on guard, ready to take captive every thought and speculation that would cause us to wander away from God and return to what is obedience to Christ.

> For though we walk in the flesh, we do not war according to the flesh, for the weapons of our warfare are not of the flesh, but divinely powerful for the destruction of fortresses. (2 Corinthians 10:3-4)

This is not referring to how well one can argue with people's faulty thinking and somehow take their thoughts captive. It's about facing our own thoughts, ideas, and attitudes when they are being drawn away from the Lord because of deteriorating conditions.

Another force that affects our work setting is the many uncertainties in the work environment, especially in these days. People, Christians included, are facing an unstable economy bringing with it job insecurity. It brings anxiety, fear, and despair, which can have a paralyzing effect on workers and their work, and the work environment becomes heavy and discouraging. Fear may not be something that energizes outward reaction, but fear spreads inwardly and fosters a repressive spirit which may debilitate employees. Recently, at a major airport, I was talking with a few airline employees whom I believe to be mature Christians. I know their hope is in the Lord, yet they would tell you how vulnerable they feel in the present work environment.

When the airline industry started its downturn after 9/11, we saw the toll it had taken on airline employees. Because many of the churches in our area have a high percentage of airline employees, we decided to organize a meeting for local pastors at the FCAP International Office. Together, we considered how their churches could be used to encourage and equip these airline people. They needed a place where they could talk and pray about how to respond to the challenges of the work environment. We also talked about how airline employees needed help in weathering the storms of the workplace, by being reinforced with the foundation of truth, which would support their faith during these though times.

Teaching them the basics of the Christian Worldview[2] will do this. It will guide their thoughts and help direct their decisions while facing these challenges. The local church should be careful not to isolate people from these problems but should insulate them with truth and hope in order to prepare them to return to their unstable work environment.

Facing the challenges of the work environment must be met with a clear understanding of how Christ is sending us back out into the world. The word pictures Christ used sheds light on the environment we are called into, and how we should see our relationship to it. Let's look at three of them, which will give us a clearer understanding of God's purpose of representing Him in our workplaces.

Like Sheep among Wolves

Reflecting on the words, "sheep among wolves," can be rather disturbing. This is not a pleasant picture and sounds dangerous. Does it mean God will be sending us into places, like the workplace, where we will feel as vulnerable sheep amongst wolves? As we look closer at this illustration, it will underscore a very basic truth about our Lord's involvement with us out in the world.

Jesus was about to commission and send out the disciples. He had told them the road ahead would be hard with difficulties and dangers. Then he used this word picture to describe His point. He said "*I am sending you, as sheep among wolves.*"[3] We all know what wolves desire to do with sheep; they want to devour them. It is known that wolves run in a pack, and they do so in order to hunt down stray sheep for food. They will even try to break up a flock of sheep by creating a commotion in order to prey on them more easily.

This peculiar picture that depicts our calling "to go out" is baffling. Sending sheep, which are weak and helpless, among wolves that run in packs waiting to devour them, sounds nothing like a pleasant and comfortable assignment. Actually, such a calling sounds troubling. However, this calling was not intended to scare the disciples or us, or to prove to the world how tough God's sheep are. Christ was painting a real picture of the ways of the world. But we are not left with this looming picture, as we are reminded... He Who is with us, is *the Great Shepherd of the sheep.*[4] When circumstances become overwhelming, we receive the power of our calling. As we declare our weakness and helplessness, we are affirming at the same time our need for God's sufficiency. Our calling to go out into the world and workplace is not to show how tough we are...but to show how almighty God is. He desires to show up in our weak and difficult circumstances.

> I can do all things through Him who strengthens me. And my God will supply all your needs according to His riches in glory in Christ Jesus. (Philippians 4:13, 19)

Ministry in the workplace is not a demonstration of human strength but God's ability to work through us in our difficult and vulnerable situation. This works, not by simply writing this truth in our notebook, or posting it on our cell phone or bedroom walls. It works when we are surrounded by people and situations that want to devour us, and we humbly acknowledge our weakness by crying out to the Great Shepherd for His assistance. His word reassures us, that when we walk through the valley of the shadow of death, we don't have to fear its evil, because He is with us.[5]

God's strategy is much different than the world's. The world wants to put on a big show of strength and power in order to display its abilities. God, on the other hand, sends His people into weak and vulnerable situations that require resources beyond their own abilities. So when you go to work, ministry will often present itself at times and in situations when it looks like those who oppose you have the upper hand. Instead of demanding God to give us the upper hand or prove to us how He will work things out, we need only to humble ourselves under His mighty hand and allow Him to lift us up in His appointed time.[6]

The Apostle Paul understood this call, depicting strength coming through weakness. In his own life He experienced how the power of Christ met him under debilitating conditions. He even boasted about his weaknesses, so that the power of Christ may dwell in him. Listen to how he applied this: *"Therefore I am well content with weaknesses, with insults, with distresses, with persecutions, with difficulties for Christ's sake, for when I am weak, then I am strong."* [7] He also described the words or message of the cross in the same way.[8] It sounds weak and lowly in the world's estimation…that one would come and claim to be king, work with his hands, serve people and ultimately give his life for his subjects and even for his enemies. It sounded utterly foolish to the world. However, the tide turned when He was raised from the dead, by the power of God. No power on earth could perform this or hold Him back. Some day the whole world will see the greatest demonstration of God's power when Christ returns. But in the meantime God is giving the world a preview of His strength through His people as they humbly draw on His enabling resources in weak and vulnerable settings.

> But we have this treasure in earthen vessels, so that the surpassing greatness of the power will be of God and not from ourselves; we are afflicted in every way, but not crushed; perplexed, but not despairing; persecuted, but not forsaken; struck down, but not destroyed; always carrying about in the body the dying of Jesus, so that the life of Jesus also may be manifested in our body. (2 Corinthians 4:7-10)

Your responding in the same way in your work environment is imperative and essential for you and your influence in the work environment. This is what authentic ministry in the workplace is all about. There are two more word pictures our Lord used to describe our calling into the world.

As Light Penetrates Darkness

This next word picture given by Jesus portrays Christians as light in dark places. He is the light of the world, and He has made us to be His lights in the world.[9] God's strategy is still the same... He is calling for light to shine out of darkness.[10] Christ calls us to be the light of the world, and not the sound of the earth. Yes, we do speak the Gospel of Christ, but according to our Lord, the character of a Christian should be that of light. There is a stark contrast between the speed of sound and the speed of light. The speed of sound travels at 786 mph, or about one mile every five seconds. In comparison, the speed of light travels at 186,282 miles per second. As you radiate the light of Christ through your actions and attitude, never underestimate the velocity and impact it has on your workplace.

The Christian faith is not to be defined in the workplace simply by how well Christians explain or describe the darkness there, but rather by how brightly their light shines in the darkness! Blessing the darkness with the light is not optional... it is the mark of our high calling as Christians. Instead of standing at a distance and being critical or angry by the dark behavior of people, we must shed the light of God's love and mercy on them in unique and creative ways.[11] Because Christ came to rescue us out of darkness and transfer us into His Kingdom of light, He sends us back into darkness to bring light to those who are caught and trapped in it. This represents our calling and ministry in the workplace.

But wait, considering the nature of light, there is another important angle to consider... It exposes the things of darkness. So, don't be surprised when you draw attention by conducting yourself in an exemplary way and doing your work commendably. It will probably be received well by some, but it can also incite frustration, resentment, and even anger in others. Why? Because diligent workers can be a threat to lazy ones, and those who cheat at work probably won't like honest coworkers either. Disgruntled employees will certainly be irritated by grateful ones. As we shine as His light, even without using words, we will be exposing the dark and sordid intentions around us.

The apostle Paul understood how dark situations could affect Christians in very real ways. He once made an appeal to the Christians in Philippi. He cautioned them to be careful not to lose their ability to shine as light by becoming complainers about the darkness around them. He even advised them not to get in disputes with people in the dark.[12] His appeal to them was to conduct their lives in an exemplary way, so that they appear as light in the midst of a crooked and perverse setting. So it is with us, when we are positioned in darkness; we have been placed there to bless it with light!

With Salt's Preserving Influence

This last word picture portrays Jesus calling us out into the world to be like salt.[13] Salt is a stable compound, which means it cannot be altered. It has the ability to change whatever it is added to, to one degree or another. The three most important ways it was used in ancient times was firstly to prevent decay by heavily salting a piece of meat. Secondly, to add flavor to dull and tasteless food, and thirdly it was used as an antiseptic to promote healing. God is sending us out into the world to preserve, bring flavor and healing in situations that are wounded, dull, and decaying. This picture of the Christian life is not about salt being presented in decorative pretty salt shakers. It's about being spread into decaying and tasteless places to bring God's influence and spiritual healing.

One of the joys I have is to hear people's stories of how they engage their faith in God out in the world. One of those stories came from Claude, a base supervisor of a major European airline. He shared with me how his airline had chosen his base, which was not the home base of the airline, to be a test run for a new stress management seminar they were thinking of endorsing. As a test for this seminar, the company made it mandatory for all employees at his base to attend. Before going to it Claude wanted to find out more about the seminar, and he discovered that it was mostly about Eastern mystic meditation, rather than offering practical help and advice. He struggled with being told he had to attend it and even thought about not going. However, after giving it some thought and prayer, he realized the importance of his influence as a Christian there. He also figured that this would give him the opportunity to listen, ask questions, and report his evaluations back to the airline headquarters. He made sure his questions would be clear and his responses gracious. He said the seminar was about having a transcendental religious experience at work but did not practically address the stressful problems at hand. This was an opportunity for Claude to be like salt, bringing God's influence into a dark situation. He reported his concerns about the lack of common sense this seminar offered and the amount of money and time the airline would waste if they endorsed it. He also offered some suggestions about ways the company could help people manage their stressful lives. The airline took Claude's suggestions seriously and the program was never adopted by the company.

We understand our calling to be the salt of the earth as we allow God to use us to bring change to tense and festering conditions. Responding God's way can be used to restrain evil as well as bring wholesomeness to our workplace.

Our potential in serving God in the workplace is not determined by how well the work environment becomes suitable to our faith, but rather how well our faith in God becomes integrated in what we do at work and how we respond to the conditions around us.

Discussion Questions

1. How are the forces (influences) around you at work putting pressure on you?
2. How does this affect your relationship with coworkers in general?
3. How can this affect your or your coworker's work performance?
4. Describe any built-in bad habits or traits that characterize your job or position?
5. Which of the three callings that Jesus depicts, as Light... as Salt... or like Sheep, resonates with you the most?
6. Describe any opportunity you have had in your workplace to be as Light... as Salt...or like Sheep.

6

WORKPLACE MINISTRY... ME?

An exciting and eye opening experience occurred in the midst of another FCAP training seminar. We had recently completed a presentation on the subject of personal ministry in the workplace. Participants were discussing and asking questions and seemed to have a handle on the information we had presented when suddenly one of them burst out, "Praise God!" At first we weren't sure why he was prompted to exclaim, "Praise God!" He paused for a minute and then continued: "I see it now... praise God, after 25 years of flying with my airline I now realize that God has given me a ministry in my workplace!" For the first time he understood that God uses ordinary people like himself to be His channels for ministry in the everyday situations of life. It had become clear to him how his work was a service to God and that the people and circumstances of work were God's appointments.

I wondered why he had not seen this before. What could have prevented him and others from realizing this? It became apparent to me as I taught more and related more to people in the workplace that a lot of people had a narrow perspective of God and the world of work. In fact there are many Christians who don't see the connection between God and personal ministry in their workplace.[1]

Holding a view that ministry is only relevant when

practiced at certain events or limited places could be drawing you away from the God-given ministry opportunities that surround you every day of your life. It was a liberating message our friend understood for the first time; he was called to be a participant in ministry right where he worked - in the midst of his everyday circumstances. I trust by the end of this chapter you will see this even more clearly and have a greater appreciation of the possibilities for ministry at your workplace.

God's Active Presence

Ministry becomes personalized in my workplace when I see myself going to an ordinary job with an extraordinary presence and power at work in me. *When God shows up at work, He does so mostly through His people.*

> I will ask the Father, and He will give you another Helper, that He may be with you forever; *that is* the Spirit of truth, whom the world cannot receive, because it does not see Him or know Him, *but* you know Him because He abides with you and will be in you. (John 14:16-17)

The disciples of Jesus saw Him perform miraculous things, and at times, they were sent by Christ to carry out such wonders themselves. However, Jesus told them in Acts 1:8 that they would need the power of His presence, the Holy Spirit, in their lives in order to fully become His witnesses. Simply experiencing God's power by observing His miraculous works was not enough. Jesus was declaring that His power would need to come from within them.

> ...But you will receive power when the Holy Spirit has come upon you; and you shall be My witnesses

> both in Jerusalem, and in all Judea and Samaria, and
> even to the remotest part of the earth. (Acts 1:8)

Like Jesus' disciples learned, we also must learn that the power of God's presence in our life can compel us to do things we naturally don't want to do. It will also restrain us from doing the wrong things we naturally would like to do. To be His witnesses in the workplace we need His restraining power to keep us from dealing with people, who treat us badly, the same way they deal with us. We also need to learn how His presence can compel us to love those who don't like us.

Oh yes, at times God will perform spectacular things to demonstrate His power. However, His active presence working through us as we perform our jobs does not bring results of lesser importance in displaying His glory. Should not the way Christians respond and act in the workplace provide a witness? God has not asked me to search for His activity in some special place or event. His treasure has been placed in me so others around me can witness His presence.[2] He personally indwells His people through the Holy Spirit so that the power of His presence can be at work in each of our lives.

Lest some of you think this is some kind of intangible mental exercise like yoga -it is not! Nor is it some kind of euphoric experience that disconnects you from work or the problems that exist there. True spirituality at the workplace does not disassociate you from the reality of what is going on around you. Rather, it creates a greater awareness of God's presence and the need of His enabling power in the midst of your current circumstances.

This truth must first take root in my own life before I can live it out and influence my surroundings. As His transforming power takes place through me, God's witness will be displayed to those around me. It is natural to just want to carry on my work as everyone else does. And yes, God does appear in the routine of our work. But, when the power of Christ's presence is working in me, the people around me will recognize that my motivation to work is driven by a greater power than that of just doing my duties. In essence we are inviting people to witness His work being done through us as we carry out our jobs. God's activity in our lives will draw greater attention in the real and raw situations of work and will bring vitality to your spiritual health.

The Ministry Agenda...Multi-Faceted

You may be wondering, should I devise a plan, a purpose statement, or some kind of ministry agenda for my workplace? No need to worry about that. God and your company have already designed that for you. Actually, God has planned your workplace agenda tailored around your job and work setting. First on the agenda is your job description - to perform it as a service first to God and also to your company. Then you'll watch it unfold as you begin to see how the people and circumstances around you are God's appointments for you. Routinely you should be asking God to open your eyes to see how He and the circumstances in your company are providing opportunities in your workplace.

God's ministry in general is multifaceted. He works in wide-ranging ways, through conversations, confrontations, or a variety of circumstances to bring people to Himself. As a Christian, take a moment and try to estimate how many different means God used to bring you to Himself. He may have used only a few or as many as one hundred different people and events in the process, and all are of equal importance. We tend to conclude that situations, like short conversations or brief encounters, are not significant enough to be considered ministry, but the opposite is true when God is at work!

A few years ago, an airline pilot, named Larry, called the FCAP International Office to share with us how he had seen God work through people around him at work. He told us that often when he flew with Christians in the cockpit, he would look for an opportunity to question or belittle their faith. He went on to say he knew that many of these Christian pilots were connected to FCAP. When he would walk through crew lounges at different airports and see FCAP publications, he would put them in the trash. But he had also noticed that many of the Christian pilots he flew with remained respectful toward him and even showed him patience and kindness when he tried to aggravate them.

Then suddenly Larry's personal circumstances went into a downward tailspin, so much so that his life seemed hopeless. During that difficult time, he kept recalling the Christian pilots with whom he had flown and how they had consistently shown him kindness. God used this to humble Larry and point him to Himself. Out of desperation, he asked God for help and subsequently recognized his need for Christ. Shortly after this, he wanted to find the Christian organization which he had so disliked, but he could not remember its name. About six months later he was in an airport crew lounge and once again found one of the FCAP publications. That is when Larry called to tell us his story. He said his reason for calling was to express his deep gratitude for the people in our ministry and share the impact they had on his life. He paused and then said, "Since coming to Christ, I wanted to contact you but didn't know how - and now that I found you, I feel like I have come home."

I've wondered if asked, how many of the Christian pilots who flew with Larry over the years considered that their time with him in the cockpit was an opportunity for ministry. Some might respond, "I had a great opportunity with a pilot who was antagonistic toward my faith." Others might say, "I had a difficult trip with a pilot who didn't like Christians." The truth is that no matter what they thought, God used each one who offered a Godly response to Larry as part of the process of bringing him to Christ. And according to Christ's words, all of them will equally receive the reward of leading Larry to Christ.

> ...So that he who sows and he who reaps may rejoice together. For in this *case* the saying is true, 'One sows and another reaps.' I sent you to reap that for which you have not labored; others have labored and you have entered into their labor. (John 4:36-38)

We should look at ministry in our workplace as both spontaneous and intentional. Engaging in both of them gives us a proper balance of workplace ministry. Let's see how!

Spontaneous Ministry

Whether you realize it or not, things will come your way unannounced on a regular basis in your work setting. The question is...do you see the potentially great value in even the small and brief encounters around you daily? God tells us that because the days have plenty of evil in them, it is important that we should be redeeming the time.

> Therefore be careful how you walk, not as unwise men but as wise, making the most of your time, because the days are evil. So then do not be foolish, but understand what the will of the Lord is. (Ephesians 5:15-17)

In this passage there are two words used for "time" in the original language. One speaks of time as a measured period, like twenty-four hours or seven days. The other word defines

WORKPLACE MINISTRY... ME?

time as an occasion that is characterized by a quality we ascribe to it. We may describe how a certain time or event was a good or a bad time. The phrase "redeem the time" uses the latter word for time, as an event or opportunity, and the word "redeem" here means literally to salvage from loss. It could be illustrated by one company buying out another company, preventing it from going into bankruptcy. Please don't miss this - it is too important! You will want to remember this as you run into difficult circumstances or challenging situations which could bring about damage or loss. You may face a coworker who is mistreating you, or perhaps you could be asked to cover up a wrong activity. When such opportunities present themselves, and it's within your ability to act, don't write them off as worthless. Instead capture the occasion by responding God's way and redeem them from loss.

The Bible instructs us to overcome evil by our responding with good.[3] This does not mean that by responding God's way the circumstances will immediately change in your favor. However, it does mean that you have invested what is good and right in a deteriorating situation.[4] By doing so, it could prevent the situation from worsening and keep you from being trapped in it. Don't let the adverse circumstances of work rob you of redeeming them; instead acknowledge God's active presence by first turning to Him in prayer.

We are told that each day has enough troubles of its own. Instead of ignoring the troubles or writing them off as worthless - redeem them! And remember, these are often the occasions God uses to lead people to Himself just as He did with Larry and those pilots.

God places great value in the small surprising situations and brief encounters with people that come our way each day. You may not have an explicit opportunity to share your faith with someone, but you can introduce your faith to people in the ways you respond to them. Jesus put great importance on the simplest gestures, even giving a cup of water to someone who at that moment is in need of it, regardless of his or her status.[5] Each of the following scenarios is a real life story that I have personally heard.

- Liz, a Flight Attendant, captures the moment when a passenger who is upset treats her harshly and is rude. Liz chooses to redeem the moment by responding kindly to him.

- Jerry, a Captain, chooses to capture the occasion of a recurring procedure when he offers to do the walk around of the plane for inspection. He redeems the moment as his first officer (whom Jerry could order to do this) is having a hard day and the weather is bad outside.

- Tim, a Mechanic, captures the moment when he hears a coworker needs help to finish his job. Tim redeems the time as he shows his willingness to go the extra mile to help his coworker even though Tim's work is completed and he could go home.

There are endless unexpected opportunities for redemption in the workplace! Next let us consider how we can engage in ministry with regularity and forethought. We can glean insight from how our Lord viewed ministry, as He and His disciples often likened it to working in a harvest.[6]

> Seeing the people, He felt compassion for them, because they were distressed and dispirited like sheep without a shepherd. Then He said to His disciples, The harvest is plentiful, but the workers are few. (Matthew 9:36-37)

Intentional Ministry

Though spontaneity is important and needed, ministry in the workplace is also intentional and developed over time. Just as sowing and cultivating are ongoing works for producing a harvest, so are the two actions necessary in Christ's workplace ministry.

We all know the importance of cultivating the ground and sowing seeds in order to reap a harvest. As we respond to the call of Jesus for us to go out into the harvest field, we realize that we cannot produce the seeds ourselves nor do we have the ability to cause them to grow. However, God does provide the spiritual seeds for the soil of human hearts. We participate in His harvesting process as we cultivate the ground He has called us to and sow His seeds.[7] Talk to any farmer, he will tell you that working for a potential harvest requires time, diligence, perseverance, and patience. One of our greatest hindrances from seeing God's harvest come to fruition is often our impatience! This will lead us to become discouraged and eventually give up.

> Let us not lose heart in doing good, for in due time we will reap if we do not grow weary. So then, while we have opportunity, let us do good to all people, and especially to those who are of the household of the faith. (Galatians 6:9-10)

As a farmer learns his trade, he learns of the different tools to use, he learns how different seeds require certain planting techniques, and he learns how to irrigate and enrich the soil. Likewise the Christian harvester must be aware of wise and effective ways to reap the rewards of the harvest.

First, let's consider good manners and habits of a wise sower in the workplace. He or she creatively and carefully sows the seeds of words, gestures, and deeds which are appropriate to the situation and at the appropriate time. The sower understands the value of simple conversations with others. Though time is precious, the sower uses time wisely and sparingly. A few well chosen Godly words are seeds sown. The wise sower has learned to do these things in ways that do not pressure people to respond.

A good friend of mine, a First Officer, told me of an interesting time he spent with a Captain on a three day trip. On the first day, as they were telling each other about themselves, it seemed as though the Captain was showing interest in hearing more about God and spiritual things. My friend thought it was an open door, so he began sharing more about his personal faith in Christ. The Captain, who up until this point was very engaged in the conversation, suddenly shut down and became silent. At first, my friend went on to tell him more, but then he realized that the Captain did not want to hear it, so he quickly and graciously backed off. For the next two days there was silence in the cockpit, except for the necessary communication to get their job done. Finally on the last day of this three-day trip, the Captain turned to my friend and said: "Now that I know you are not going to push this stuff on me, I would like to pick up the conversation about God." You see, a good sower depends on the work of the Holy Spirit and does not push or force the seed into the ground.

Another trait of a good sower is to know which seed works best in what type of soil. For example, when situations at work are discouraging and even despairing, seeds of hope are needed. Discouraged hearts need to be met with compassionate and discerning words, not just a kind benediction. These good seeds will come forth from people who live their lives in complete dependence on God in all situations. You cannot give hope to people if your life is full of anxiety and frustration. But, you can pass on hope and compassion, when in troubles you are being comforted by the God of all comfort.[8]

Some of our FCAP staff are involved with the airport chaplaincy and hold regular meetings with airlines people during their layovers or breaks. They usually look at a Bible passage and share some thoughts that apply to their work settings and then pray for one another and their company. One day there were two ladies who had come to one of these meetings for the first time. At the end of the prayer time they spoke up and shared why they had decided to come to the meeting. They pointed to one of their coworkers who was also there and attended regularly and said: "We came today because we want what she has." Their airline was going through some turbulent changes, and evidently this lady's faith and conduct was spreading seeds about the God of all hope which was directing them to our Lord.

Now let's look at the qualities of a good cultivator. One of the key factors is that of becoming a good neighbor to those around you at work. Our coworkers are like our neighbors at work with whom we rub shoulders daily. Thus we need to be giving a great deal of attention to these relationships. The following words of Jesus are profoundly practical and real and speak to us about ministry in the harvest. The great command Jesus gave his followers was to first love the Lord your God and then to love your neighbor as you would yourself. As Christians we cannot escape these words of our Lord.

To be a good neighbor to your coworkers means to learn to identify with their spiritual, physical, and material needs. Are there coworkers around you who are in need? Perhaps you know someone who is struggling with making ends meet financially, or maybe they are in a difficult relationship with their spouse or children. Others may be experiencing physical illness or have someone in their family who is suffering. People involved in God's harvest become accustomed to using their personal resources (time, money, talents) to show people around them the compassion and kindness of God. Sowing such seeds can have a long-lasting affect and can produce quite a harvest.

Here is how a friend of ours (flight attendant) did this in a simple way. When flight attendants are newly hired, they are paid a lower scale pay for a specified time. Many of them find it hard to make ends meet during this time. When our friend, who has flown for years, flies with one of these new hires, she looks for opportunities to bless them by taking them out and paying for their meal on their layovers. By cultivating the harvest field of your workplace and spreading God's seeds there, you are uniquely showing people who God is and how He works.

The founder of FCAP is a retired airline pilot who invested his life in workplace ministry for over 40 years now. Joe Ivey is not only a good friend of mine but also a partner in ministry. When I became the director of FCAP in 1992, Joe was retiring from flying, but he has yet to retire from investing in people's lives, especially those in the airline workplace. He would tell you how God placed a burden on his heart for every pilot in his airline early one morning in 1971. At that time, when he would walk through the pilot lounge in Atlanta, he knew of only a few other Christians in his company. Joe saw the need for Christians to identify with each other, so he started simply meeting with a handful of pilots. He and his wife, Barbara, began investing their time and resources by praying, meeting, and encouraging others in his workplace and eventually in other airlines. Within one year a Flight Attendant named Janice Barfield had a burden for her fellow flight attendants, and God used her to form this part of the ministry in FCAP. Soon after this, airline ground personnel also started forming ministry groups in their area. The ministry spread to different cities and eventually around the world. If you had the opportunity to sit down with Joe, he could tell you one story after another of how God turned ordinary connections with people in the workplace into wonderful ministry opportunities. He was respected by his company and fellow coworkers for the way he did his work and how he had a genuine interest in the people around him. Prior to his retirement he told us there was not one day when he'd be walking through the pilot lounge that he wouldn't be approached by at least one other Christian pilot, and they would fellowship together. Joe hasn't stopped ministering to airline people. Now in his retirement he is heading up his airline's retired pilots monthly meeting in Atlanta where, again, he looks for opportunities to maintain relationships. He continues to be an example of investing his life in people.

Sadly, there are Christians who will spend 90,000+ hours of their lives in the workplace and never see the possibilities for ministry in God's spiritual harvest. Faith in the workplace must be more than a private spiritual reflection which occurs at a secluded moment in the workday. Faith in the workplace means I engage it by demonstrating my relationship with God and my confidence and trust in Him to the people and in situations around me. Ask yourself right now...In what way am I willing to trust God to use me at my workplace today? You cannot expect to enjoy the reward of God's harvest some day without seeing yourself involved with Him in it now. However, when you take steps of faith to sow and cultivate your workplace, it will transform its landscape from one of spiritual barrenness to one of spiritual fruitfulness!

Often when people contact FCAP we hear them say that their schedule is too full for them to be involved in ministry. We respond by saying..."*We do not ask you to add more events to your busy work schedule but to capitalize on the opportunities already existing there.*" What unique opportunities exist in your workplace? How can you capitalize on this fertile soil?

Discussion Questions

1. Have you ever considered how your job description is part of God's agenda for your ministry at work? Are you inspired or daunted to hear that?

2. God's presence in our life is said to bring both a compelling and restraining influence to our lives. What effects should this have in your workplace?

3. Name some ways you need God to compel you at work.

4. Also, name some ways you need Him to restrain you at work.

5. If God's ministry agenda unfolds as we see people and circumstances around us to be His appointments, what hinders me from seeing them in my workplace?

6. If God places great value on the little things going on around us, could there be any current opportunities in your workplace that you could possibly be missing?

RESPONDING
TO WORKPLACE
CONDITIONS

WHEN
GOD
SHOWS UP AT
WORK

7

HAVING A
PROACTIVE FAITH

I would like you to meet Tom. If we were to ask Tom about his faith, he would not hesitate to tell us that he is a Christian who is regularly involved in a church. He also teaches a Sunday school class. But if asked, he would also let us know that he struggles with living out his faith at the workplace. Why? Tom is working with a person who lives a moral lifestyle quite opposite from Tom's. In fact, Tom's coworker flaunts the questionable lifestyle and is very outspoken about it. Tom finds himself in a dilemma; somehow he would like to give his coworker a piece of his mind, but instead Tom has resorted to being cool and aloof toward him.

Tom feels if he ignores this person long enough, the tension will gradually go away, but to the contrary; Tom's resentment toward this person only increases. Tom seems powerless as his faith becomes paralyzed and he no longer knows what to do. He wonders if praying against his enemies would be an effective way to deal with this situation. Then he recalls the words of Jesus, when He said: *"Bless those who curse you and pray for those who mistreat you."* [1]

Martha loves going to church on Sunday. She finds great encouragement and direction in her faith when she is there. The people of the church love her, and Martha feels comforted and accepted by them. She appreciates and embraces them as well.

However, when Martha enters her workplace she feels everything but love and comfort. Her company cut her pay after 18 years of service, and she is hearing rumors that some of the company's upper management are taking bonuses. The tensions at work are growing daily from anxiety, fear, disappointment, and anger. The general attitude is depressing and deteriorating. Martha experiences spiritual paralysis and cannot wait to leave work every day.

In the two examples of Tom and Martha, we see the vast contrast between ministry conditions in the workplace and those in a local church setting. In our local churches we feel comfortable in the controlled environment. Our faith is protected and encouraged as we gather with likeminded people. However, the conditions of the workplace affect our faith quite differently. Spiritually, the atmosphere feels almost out of control because we face resistance, rejection, and worldly habits. Certainly Tom and Martha felt the pressures of their conditions in the workplace. For all practical purposes those burdens paralyzed their faith.

Workplace conditions are not just created by how well or how poorly employees perform their jobs; there are many facets that affect the work environment (good and bad ones). The setting can become quite negative when clashes occur over conflicting attitudes, morals, values, and work practices. And certainly the array of personality traits impacts the conditions at work.

Here are a few problematic conditions that tend to recur in the workplace and put pressure on us:

- Criticism and insults from coworkers and supervisors
- Diverse ethical and moral values among coworkers
- People resorting to gossip and slander
- Company policies that seem cold hearted and unfair
- Selfishness and greed

- Harsh and demeaning communication
- Preferential treatment for certain people or groups

Consider Your Response

You respond in at least one of three ways to the conditions around you at work. You may try to IGNORE IT. You ignore a conflicting situation when you choose to turn away from the problem or person by refusing to admit there is a problem. Giving a "cold shoulder" when facing problems, communicates your unwillingness to resolve them.[2]

You could choose to REACT TO IT; reaction here meaning in an impulsive, aggressive way. You do this when you take the role of the adversary by quickly labeling people as your enemy when they cross you the wrong way. You find it easy to argue with them or oppose them, treating them as you deem they deserve or by how they have treated you.

Or, you may respond by ENGAGING IN IT. Your faith is engaged in workplace conditions when you apply it in the situations with people and circumstances at work. The notion that faith is not engaged unless it is by way of witnessing is not uncommon. However, faith is practically engaged when the Gospel is demonstrated in the tough conditions of work. In other words, we act out the Gospel by treating people with whom we clash, the way we have been treated by Jesus Christ. We have been shown grace and mercy and our sins have been forgiven. If it is said, that God is using us to make His appeal to people to be reconciled to Him, thus we should be showing that reconciliation as part of our response.

In order to exemplify reconciliation we, as Christians, must become more proactive in our walk of faith throughout our workday. The term proactive means anticipating problems and taking affirmative steps to prepare ourselves, so when we face adverse situations, we know how to respond. The Bible gives us a clear description of the condition of our world, the state of the human heart, and what liberates both of them. These truths can guide our hearts to respond to the adverse conditions in Godly ways. In contrast, the lack of preparedness can result in damaging reactions which can cause lasting emotional turmoil. *Our faith and obedience to our Lord in responding to adverse conditions is imperative and prevents us from being soured and contaminated.*

Now we will consider some ways we can prepare ourselves to meet the challenges of workplace conditions.

Spiritual Emergency Procedure

The airline industry goes to great lengths and cost to prepare its people with emergency response procedures. They do this so their people will be prepared to respond quickly and effectively when the unexpected happens. The value of this training comes from written classroom instructions and from the hands-on repeated exercises in mock scenarios. As employees practice and apply the written material, the emergency procedures become second nature to them.

At one of our FCAP conferences in India, I asked Lav Samuels, Captain with Air India and a very dear friend of mine, to stand next to me and pretend he was in the cockpit flying a trip. Here is the scenario, "Suddenly the warning lights and alerts are coming on informing you that number two engine is failing. What is your reaction?" Like clockwork he demonstrated what he had practiced so many times during his career. The "Standard Operating Procedure" that would prepare the crew and passengers for such an emergency had become second nature to him.

In a similar way, we can prepare ourselves to respond in a Godly way when we are faced with unexpected circumstances.

How? We first begin by looking at and learning God's prescribed Biblical responses. In His Word, God has given us plenty of practical examples of real life scenarios on how to respond His way. It takes more than just memorizing such passages; it means to learn and apply them in our current problematic situations.[3] The lack of this application could have been what hindered Tom's and Martha's ability to live out their faith at their workplace.

Having a proactive faith does not eliminate problems, but it does shape our lives and may positively affect the people around us. Let us look at some important spiritual emergency responses that will prepare us to respond appropriately when unexpected situations arise at our work.

Alert to Pray

A response to pray was of utmost importance to Jesus Christ. His life demonstrated this while He was on earth. At times He even removed Himself for periods of time to pray. This urgency to engage in prayer is found throughout the Bible. In Luke 18:1, Jesus told His followers that they should pray in all things instead of becoming fearful and disheartened. When Jesus faced His greatest earthly trial of being arrested, tried, and crucified, He told His followers: *"Pray that you may not enter into temptation."*[4]

Often people think they need to join a prayer meeting or at least be in the presence of certain people in order to pray. But Jesus calls us to pray at all times. Praying should be as automatic to our spiritual life as breathing is to our physical life.[5] Prayer is more than a devotional or ecclesiastical ritual performed on a scheduled day or at a special location by certain people. It is the privilege of every Christian to talk personally with God, our Heavenly Father, about everything and anything! When we engage in prayer in every situation of life, we declare our dependence on God. We humbly acknowledge in faith our need for Him to guide, to provide, and to sustain us. You, like me, most likely have heard the comment, "Well, at least we can pray." We should be saying, "We can pray...it's the most effective thing we can do!" Please know, if you don't see how praying engages your faith in difficulties you will resort to other, less effective means.

What is your first response when crisis hits your workplace? Have you trained yourself to be alert by first running to God? This is not a suggestion! We are instructed to be alert by praying for the things happening around us.

> With all prayer and petition pray at all times in the Spirit, and with this in view, be on the alert with all perseverance and petition for all the saints...
> (Ephesians 6:18)

As you practice this privilege in your workplace, or any place for that matter, you will find peace, stability, strength, hope, wisdom, and guidance even in the most trying situations. God loves to hear our prayers of faith because He wants to be involved in the details of our life. I believe one of the reasons why God allows difficulties in our lives is for us to learn to trust Him and be alert to pray in all things.[6] Rather than seeing prayer as some kind of "magic wand" that will change the circumstances immediately, we can be assured that God will use our prayer to change us and to supply what is needed at the moment. There is so much more that could be said on prayer, but let me urge you to take advantage of this direct "life line" to the One who holds all things in His hands!

> Be anxious for nothing, but in everything by prayer
> and supplication with thanksgiving let your requests

be made known to God. And the peace of God, which surpasses all comprehension, will guard your hearts and your minds in Christ Jesus. (Philippians 4:6-7)

I enjoy hearing stories of how people have experienced peace and strength in the inner sanctuary of their soul by turning to God in prayer when everything around them was chaotic and confusing. Liz (flight attendant) has led a training session for us that deals with how to respond to unreasonable people. She often shares a very practical routine she applies when facing complaining passengers, quarrelsome coworkers, or just feels faint and ready to give in when things get out of control. To help her take a timeout to pray, she purposefully lets her pen drop to the floor. While she bends down to pick it back up, she takes the opportunity to call out to God for help. She says: "It's amazing how this practice helps me to regain my focus and prepares me for what is ahead, keeping my thoughts and attitude on the right course."

Do the difficulties of work draw you toward God or away from Him? Why not give some thought to creating a routine in your workday that would remind you to be on the alert to pray in all things. You might want to also consider asking a few coworkers if they would like to meet with you for prayer during a break time. Though we are called to pray at all times, collective prayer is often a great source of encouragement and support.

Once we have prayed, some situations require more thought and time. Thus we need to consider how we rehearse the responses conceived in our hearts.

The Dress Rehearsal

Have you ever been asked to play a role? If yes, you were probably given a script which you had to memorize. Then you started acting out the part, and the more you rehearsed the more you added emphasis through body language, voice inflections, and emotions. The more you became vocally and physically involved, the more your character became real and believable. In a similar way, all of us eventually live out what we rehearse in our hearts. Tom and Martha (mentioned earlier in this chapter) may have thought that they could escape the reality of their work surroundings by not responding to them. But whether they realized it or not, their work setting was affecting them, and they were rehearsing the part of "choosing to ignore". As humans, we continually process the things that are going on around us mentally and emotionally which affect our thoughts, views, and outlook about life and those around us. These emotions may cause us to rehearse the role of "confrontation and attack". Perhaps we have clashed with someone at work. In a disagreement, unkind and hurtful words are often spoken. Such words can leave the scene frigid and awkward. You play the scenario over and over in your mind trying to justify your side of it. You may start thinking that you need to prove your point and give others a piece of your mind. The more you rehearse the part the more it escalates and you are setting yourself up for failure. Why? Because you will probably act out what you have rehearsed. If you relive responses with bitterness, anger, or sarcastic thoughts, they will reflect in your communications, both verbally and physically.

God instructs us to renew our minds continually, "...*and do not be conformed to this world, but be transformed by the renewing of your mind.*"[7] The word for "renew" brings out the idea of exchange. We cannot expect to walk into the workplace with our hearts full of anger and slander, and then hope to have kind words and gracious actions flow from us. Though we may not have control over circumstances, we do have control over what we choose to think about and to dwell upon.[8] God directs us to consider learning His thoughts and ways which are far superior to ours.

> "For My thoughts are not your thoughts, nor are your ways My ways," declares the LORD. "For *as* the heavens are higher than the earth, So are My ways higher than your ways and My thoughts than your thoughts." (Isaiah 55:8-9)

This is called the true wisdom that comes from above, and when applied to our work condition, it teaches us to act wisely and gently.[9] Let's see how we can further prepare ourselves to respond wisely to our workplace conditions.

Responding by What You Know

When aviators encounter dangerous weather, they first identify their location in relation to the storms in order to navigate around them. Because pilots have no visible intersections at 35,000 feet with street signs, they use coordinates to identify their location and movement (coordinates give us longitude, latitude, and altitude). The pilots then reroute their flight based on what they know; not on what they don't know. In other words, in a situation like this you would not want a pilot who gets distracted by trying to figure out where the storm came from or how long it will last or even try to guess if he could fly through it. You want a pilot who makes his decisions based on the facts he knows to be reliable and dependable and recalculates the flight path to divert away from potential danger.

This example offers some helpful parallels for us to examine as we respond to the turbulent conditions at our workplace. First, we can ask ourselves if we are aware of the changing circumstances around us, and then evaluate how to proceed. Do we handle them by what we know, or do we try to figure out the unknowns?

In the Bible, God has given us His coordinates by which to live our lives. When we learn these and apply them, they will safely guide us through all weather conditions of life. Conflicts at work can appear like storms on the horizon. If we are not careful, they can quickly divert our attention away from God. We get tempted to fix our attention on the unknown and become confused and lost, at which point we start making decisions based on our instincts. Without God and His prescribed coordinates, the volatile conditions around us will take us off course.

Trying to fathom people's motives and reasoning is not wrong. However, becoming preoccupied with them could delay you from doing what you already know would be the right thing to do. In fact, this can be costly, consuming much of your time and energy. I have witnessed this in people who have tried to interpret difficult workplace situations. Some have even claimed that God gave them a word of revelation, while at the same time neglecting to apply His principles which directly relate to their circumstances.

The truth of God's Word provides practical application to all of life's situations. Simply knowing about them is not enough, as the power of God's Word becomes evident in those who take steps of faith. Here is a list of some of God's principles that act as coordinates, directing us on the right heading:

- Pray for our enemies instead of allowing ourselves to react and be overcome by their evil. Overcome evil with good! (Romans 12:21)
- Look for ways to love those who don't love or like you. (Matthew 5:43-44)
- Be slow to speak and quick to listen because it is easy for our tongue to quickly say the wrong things. (James 1:19)

- We are told not to look out for our own interest only, but also for the interest of others. (Philippians 2:3-4)
- When opportunities arise we should be willing to do more than what is expected of us by going the extra mile. (Matthew 5:41)
- Knowing the truth is one thing, but speaking the truth in a kind and loving way in difficult situations is just as important. (Ephesians 4:15)
- Forgive as Christ has forgiven you (Colossians 3:13). Forgiveness should characterize us and influence our response toward difficult people. If it doesn't, we can be tempted to harbor unforgiveness.
- Let your yes be yes, and no be no, because everything else leads to confusion. (Matthew 5:37; James 5:12

Do these sound too simplistic? It may be because they are profoundly simple. Like coordinates, they give us a sense of where we stand spiritually when conditions are pressing in on us to take a wrong turn. I also must ask myself: "Am I navigating on God's GPS (God's Positioning System) or my own?" God's GPS may not change the adverse conditions surrounding me, but His system will protect me from sliding into worse conditions filled with anger, bitterness, and resentment. Be careful not to trivialize the value of these coordinates, especially as you are navigating through the storms of the workplace.

Take a moment to evaluate some ongoing, challenging conditions in your workplace. Be aware of the traits, attitudes, and ideas that make up your work environment. Now ask yourself: "How are these affecting me emotionally?" and "How am I responding to them?" We have talked about you becoming proactive in your faith at work. With this in mind think about some practical steps you could take to apply these in your surroundings at work. Responding to workplace conditions entails preparation and rehearsal of the part you will play in the scenarios of your workplace.

DISCUSSION QUESTIONS

1. How do you see the conditions at church favorable for ministry? In comparison, how do you see the conditions at the workplace unfavorable and challenging for ministry?

2. Evaluate your work environment and think about your relational interactions with your coworkers. Consider how the three different approaches "Ignore it, React to it, Engage in it" are affecting your coworkers and yourself.

3. Describe a difficult situation that happened in your workplace. How did your coworkers respond to it? How did you respond to it?

4. Looking back at the section "Responding by What You Know," - what are some prescribed responses from God's Word that could be applied to difficult situations at your work?

5. Evaluate your prayer life at work... how would you and your workplace benefit from you praying spontaneously and intentionally about the things going on there?

6. Events and difficulties amongst coworkers often cause us to have inner turmoil, in which we ponder and rehearse our responses. Describe how such a rehearsal can go in a wrong direction. How can you steer it to go in a right direction?

7. Name some precepts or principles from God's Word that would be important and helpful to have stored in your heart as you enter the workplace.

8

RULES OF ENGAGEMENT

We had an airline employee attend one of our seminars who worked in the lost luggage department. As she introduced herself and her job, I thought to myself: "She must work in an interesting environment!" She described how stressful her job was. Almost daily people would walk up to the counter in a tirade, accusing her of losing their things and messing up their travel plans. As angry words and threats would cause the atmosphere to become tense and even combative, she would find it harder to respond in a proper manner. This was not only difficult from a professional standpoint, but as a Christian she knew returning anger with anger was a poor example of her faith. She realized how easily she could be drawn into using the same battle tactics that were being used on her. It was important to her that she would not adopt those ways but take a wise and more Biblical approach in her responses.

The term *"Rules of Engagement"* is a code of conduct designed to govern the use of force during warfare in order to prevent escalation of a situation. These rules are not so much about attack strategies as they are guidelines that restrict the abuse of force.

Our friend in the lost baggage department was in need of some "rules of engagement" for handling the difficult customers. As a group we discussed what measures would be best for her to follow in her work. Our suggestion was for her to first pray, acknowledging her need of God's help, then to genuinely identify with the passenger's pain at the loss of his luggage and offer sincere apologies. The passenger might show his frustration and rage, but she should then kindly proceed to explain how the airline would rectify the problem in a cooperative way. If, at this point, the passenger would still continue to express his anger and threats, she should calmly, yet firmly, inform him that if he preferred to have the airport police help solve the matter she would call on them. Since then, this lady has shared with us that although these irate passengers still show up, the "rules of engagement" that we had discussed were helping her to handle these situations in a more agreeable way. On a side note, the way the group at our training discussed and evaluated this lady's challenges is a good example of how Christians should be supporting one another in the workplace.

The basic ingredients for conflicts are people and problems for which the workplace provides a favorable breeding ground. When conflicts arise, they usually do so because there is a *"difference in opinion and purpose that frustrates someone's goal or desires."* [1] God's approach to dealing with conflict and problems is different from the world's approach. In His Word, He has spelled out ways for us to engage with difficult people and difficult situations. Approaching conflict God's way and not ours is another way **God shows up in our work.**

God's Approach

When we talk about "approach" we mean how we come across to one another. When we are working with people we like and all is going well, it is easy to approach people in a reciprocating way. The Bible tells us it's easy to love those who love us but goes on to say there is nothing exceptional about that.[2] But when we show love to those who don't like us or those with whom we are in conflict, we bear the likeness of our Heavenly Father.

> But love your enemies, and do good, and lend, expecting nothing in return; and your reward will be great, and you will be sons of the Most High; for He Himself is kind to ungrateful and evil *men*. (Luke 6:35)

How are you coming across to your coworker who differs from your moral and ethical views or with whom you have a conflict? What are your tone of voice, your body language, and gestures conveying? Is it frustration, coldness, and dislike, or is it patience, concern, and love? We are told in the Bible that as a person thinks in his or her heart, so they are in real life.[3] That being true, we need to examine our hearts in order to evaluate how we come across to our coworkers, especially those who are different from us.

The Fallout of Basic Instinct

All of us have a natural desire to have the "upper hand" when conflicts arise. This built-in instinct can work to our good when applied in life threatening situations. However, it tends to create fallout and complicate circumstances when we take this position in working out problems with people. The desire to be right or to be the winner ends up being the driving force in resolving the matter. Typically, such an approach goes like this - we concisely and passionately point out our adversary by exposing his or her wrong motives and actions, while making ourselves look as good a possible. We also see this technique used in our legal system. Each side seeks to win the case by defeating the other side and usually shows no interest in taking steps to restore damaged and broken relationships. Our news media do it this way; when reporting a story about two opposing sides, they focus almost entirely on their differences and say little or nothing about a solution. Acting solely on our basic instinct in working out problems falls far too short of God's approach!

Start with Whom?

"Me? ...part of the problem? No way, I did nothing to cause this!" Isn't this another natural tendency we have – the other person is entirely at fault; not me!

Jesus' approach to resolve conflicts and problems is to take a good look at myself first. To ask myself: "Have I contributed anything to cause the problem, or am I in any way prolonging its resolve?" Jesus instructs us to start with ourselves. Even though I may be 70% right and only 30% wrong, I must start by examining my own heart first. *"You hypocrite, first take the log out of your own eye, and then you will see clearly."*[4]

The other person's fault does not cancel out my resentment, anger, or cutting response. God's approach means that no matter how little or how much I have contributed to creating or prolonging the conflict, I start by examining myself. This will free me to look at my opponent through the eyes of Christ. As I practice this, I will realize that I too am in need of forgiveness, and that I have been forgiven much. This will enable me to open my heart to forgive others.

How You Say It

Isn't it amazing that everything can seem to be going just fine when suddenly, out of nowhere, a conversation turns sour as sarcastic and cutting words multiply like a fire storm? A close friend from my school days used to tell me that knowing what is right is only 50%; the other 50% is how I communicate what is right in a kind and loving way without manipulation or condescension. Conveying what needs to be said in an acceptable way is often where we fail in our dealings with people.

It is known that communication entails words, tone of voice, and body language or gestures. But are we aware that words can have the least impact when all three are part of the conversation? I don't think I could convince you that I was sorry about something if I told you so in an antagonistic tone with my arms crossed over my chest, while looking the other way.

God stresses the importance of the way things are said, for He instructs us to *"Let your gentle spirit be known to all men. The Lord is near."*[5] Right wording is important, but communicating the words in a compassionate way encourages mutual understanding and mutual respect.[6]

Inviting Participation

In order to approach a conflict, steps need to be taken, but who should take the first one? Another one of our natural tendencies is to dig in our heels and expect our opponent to take the first step. When we dig in, we communicate that the other person has committed the greater offense, and it's not up to us to make the first move. Sometimes people are fearful to make the first move or just don't know how to make that first step. Interestingly, the Bible tells Christians, whether they are the offender or the offended, they should be willing to take the first step.[7]

I learned something years ago that has been a great help to me in approaching people with whom I am in conflict. When something needs ironing out between me and another person, I first approach them by acknowledging the problem and then admit I need their help in the matter. Here is how I ask: "I know this or that has happened and I would like to see us resolve it, but I need your help to work it out. Would you help me, please?" In most instances my attitude of mutual cooperation begins the process of working together toward a solution.

Get Off Your Pedestal!

Positional bargaining is when I state my position at the outset. I let my opponent know my views and opinions about the conflict before giving him or her a chance to explain his or her side. At the same time I let him or her know what I am willing to do and what I will not do in regard to a possible concession. Here is another natural tendency we lean toward. We feel if we position ourselves, passionately defending our viewpoint upfront without hearing the other side, we will have a better chance to win. What we really are communicating when taking this approach is – that our side of the story is of greater significance than the other one's; and that it is more important to hear us out first before the other side is permitted to speak. This approach can also pressure people into making concessions without allowing further discussion. God's approach is one that encourages mutual respect for and from each side. He instructs us to "...be quick to hear, slow to speak and slow to anger; for the anger of man does not achieve the righteousness of God."[8]

We can encourage mutual listening and timely communication by asking each other questions. A good rule for engagement is not to ask rhetorical questions. These are questions that are asked in order to make a point without really expecting a reply. Good questions uncover facts that can help understand the other person's view or important details to help bring resolve. Another way to be "quick to listen" is to ask the other person to define the problem of the conflict from their point of view. The best positioning is when both sides see themselves on equal ground.

Common Interests, Please!

Identifying common interests first is helpful when both sides have acknowledged the problem and begin working on resolving it. A common interest is something that both sides of the conflict deem as important and can use together in working out their differences. It is not the final solution, but it is helpful for taking steps to progress toward the common goal of resolution.

This story may seem simple but it will serve as example. Several office workers are using a refrigerator in the break room for their lunches, snacks, drinks, etc. Some of them are careless by leaving their leftover foods to rot and they don't clean up spills. Other office workers want to keep the fridge clean and organized. These differing habits have caused friction among the employees and they complain to each other. The office manager becomes aware of the situation and is annoyed that adults are making a fuss over such a matter. To solve the problem quickly, he tells them: "I recommend that you figure out how you can manage this together, or we will get rid of the fridge." Since all of the employees like the convenience of having a refrigerator; they now have a common interest in respectfully solving the refrigerator problem for everyone.

God's approach instructs us to identify with the interest of others and to treat them as equally important as our own.

> Do nothing from selfishness or empty conceit, but with humility of mind regard one another as more important than yourselves; do not *merely* look out for your own personal interests, but also for the interests of others. (Philippians 2:3-4)

Such common interests are not always easily spelled out, but are worth spending time to discover.

Conquering Love

What do we do in a conflict when communications have come to a halt or when it seems the other side wants to make life miserable for us? Our natural tendency is to return the same treatment as we are receiving. Once again, God's approach is very different and may seem impossible for us to follow. And it is! Loving those who despise us and are willing to hurt us is not a natural human trait. It is supernatural and requires us to take steps of faith to trust God and look to Him to provide the spiritual and emotional strength. *"Overcoming evil with good,"*⁹ requires us to be focused and deliberate on how we will return love. The most obvious first step is to pray for all concerned, as instructed by our Lord.

Careful! We should not abuse this charge by shoving good deeds obnoxiously on those who don't like us or by being "painfully sweet" to such people to get back at them. There are appointed times to show genuine kindness toward people who don't care for us, just as there are times we should not bother them. A dear friend of ours (we'll call him Jay), who works in a key position at an airport, shared with us how his boss did not like him because he was a Christian. This boss would make cutting remarks about Jay's faith, belittling things personally dear to him. This created a difficult working environment filled with tension and friction. As our friend tried to remain kind and respond with small acts of kindness, Jay's boss would only grow more antagonistic toward him. Jay then decided it would probably be best to just continue doing his work the best he could and communicate solely on a professional basis with her. Then one day this supervisor experienced a death in her family.

Jay approached her and offered to step in and do extra necessary work at the office, so she could attend to the family. Our friend found out that God provides the appropriate time to show kindness and to do good. Jay's boss later acknowledged Jay's thoughtfulness and offered much gratitude.[10]

Having considered some of these "rules of engagement", we must also be aware that the Bible does not tell us we must make peace with everyone. It instructs us – *if possible, so far as it depends on you, be at peace with everyone.*[11] Thus, we should always be willing to make peace but we cannot force it. Don't let difficult people and battles at work rob you of an opportunity to demonstrate God's power and presence through your life. Applying His "rules of engagement" is one of the ways **God shows up** through you in your workplace!

Mastering Leadership

Finally, I would like to turn our attention to those in positions of authority. God's instructions are no different for supervisors, managers, executives, and business owners. All that we have talked about applies to them as well. However, the Bible reveals that people in these positions are given abilities to bring changes into the work environment in ways others cannot. God's Word tells the ones in authority to "grant" justice and fairness to those under them. The word "grant" here carries the idea to "render from one's own part or resources". It assumes certain people have the capability of providing an environment of fairness and justice to those who are under their authority. In Ephesians chapter 6, masters were told to stop threatening their servants, but treat them as they would treat themselves, without showing partiality.[12] In that era, this view was exceptional and unheard of, since slaves under the Roman law had no rights. Christian masters were not simply encouraged to show acts of charity or hand out gifts and bonuses, but rather they were charged to provide, by the authority invested in their position, a just and fair setting at work. The reason being, that masters would someday give an account of how they treated people under them. Christians who are in positions of authority today are called to do the same.

Engaging in Leadership

The instruction God gives to those in positions of authority is practical and challenges some natural tendency. One tendency is to show favoritism to certain people or certain groups in the workplace. Such preferential treatment can cause confusion, send wrong signals to employees, and alter the ways employees relate to one another and to those in leadership. The temptation for employees can be to "butter up" to their supervisors to gain a better standing at work. This, in turn, minimizes the importance of employee character and merits of work. Such behavior is not uncommon in a work environment where favoritism is tolerated. Instead of employees taking responsibility to work out the problems amongst each other, each side tries to "chum up" to the ones in authority. Another way partiality appears in the work environment is when company policy is not applied consistently. A supervisor is fostering favoritism when he continually allows employees to violate a seemingly insignificant company regulation, but then suddenly decides to apply it to an employee he does not like. I know of a hard-working, dedicated airline employee with impeccable work ethics who hung a notice on a bulletin board with an encouraging thought and scripture about work. Although company policy stated that this board was only to be used for company notices and announcements, it had always been used by employees to post other notifications. No one ever seemed to mind and the policy was never reinforced. Until suddenly, one day, this employee's supervisor got so irritated at this posting that he filed a complaint. This ultimately led to the employee being reprimanded by upper management and receiving a warning.

People in positions of authority who show and allow partiality to individuals or groups are setting the stage for future conflict within that environment. Preferential treatment builds dividing walls and fosters animosity among individuals and groups. God instructs those in authority not to show partiality but to provide equal footing for all employees. This does not imply that all positions are equal, but that the company and its leadership are equally fair and just in their dealing with everyone.

There are ways to encourage a fair and just work environment. A written policy with practical procedures that spell out how good relationships are maintained can be helpful. Such a policy might describe guidelines for healthy communications while also addressing wrong tactics which can be demeaning and maligning. It is important to provide clear procedures for handling conflicts between employees. These will prepare the employee to know how to act and how to proceed when conflicts arise. The guidelines should encourage the ones involved in the conflict to assume responsibility to work together toward a solution. God's way of handling conflicts is to contain the fallout as much as possible by starting with the two parties involved and only bring in others when needed.[13] Additional steps and consequences should be spelled out when there is resistance to cooperating by one or both sides. The best of company policies and procedures cannot replace the leadership's role model for displaying and living these out themselves. I once experienced a surprising opportunity that came through one of our FCAP groups. A few pilots had a genuine concern about ongoing relational problems among their fellow pilots and their union. In order to prevent the situation from deteriorating further, they appealed to their union and asked to meet in order to discuss possible solutions. They also asked if I could join them to offer some guidelines for conflict resolution. At that meeting I heard the union leaders express how they desired better communications and relationships between their pilots and with the company. After the second meeting, we watched the union leadership embrace the idea of creating a healthier approach in dealing with the company. As they began modeling good relationships, doors of communications opened and the company and union had the most profitable exchange in its history.

This was another example to me of the impact Christians can have in their workplace when they are willing to engage their faith God's way. As Christians, whether or not our company provides guidelines and procedures, we have God's "rules of engagement" which guide our responses through conflicts in the right way. By following God's "rules" we will set examples to coworkers as well as to those in leadership positions.

DISCUSSION QUESTIONS

1. If it was in your power to do so… what steps could you take to limit the escalation of an explosive conflict in your workplace?
2. Write down some ways that "gentleness" can be incorporated in your workplace.
3. A conflict arises with a co-worker over a different point of view in handling a procedure. Write down some questions you could ask him/her that would encourage mutual respect and cooperation.

4. You are in a conflict with your coworker; what are some "common interests" that you could focus on that would encourage both of you to proceed in resolving the conflict?

5. Showing deliberate, focused love toward those who despise you can be done in a right and wrong way. Give some examples of how deliberate, focused love could be misunderstood by the one receiving it.

6. As a leader in your workplace (or future one), what are some important guiding principles from God's Word that you believe would shape and influence the work environment under your leadership?

9

GOD'S BIGGER PICTURE

Jeff, a young man, was comfortable in an airline management career that offered him security and promised a great future. He enjoyed his work and working with people, but all of that changed one day. Jeff's stable company was forced to restructure and eliminate jobs due to globalization within the airlines. Overnight, it seemed as though Jeff's work turned from a satisfying profession into a difficult job. Employees became fearful and began creatively fighting to keep their jobs. In the midst of this battle, the leadership approached Jeff informing him that he would be losing his position. Then Jeff was told that he would be responsible to train the person who would replace him. The situation was mortifying for Jeff. Others who also lost their jobs were expressing their disappointments and resentments in various ways. As a Christian, Jeff knew God's guidelines and he did not want resentment and vengeance to be part of the way he would engage his faith in this difficult circumstance. In the midst of his agony, Jeff and I talked over the phone. Putting his trust in God he told me, "If this is my last month, it will be my best month for the company." Jeff did give his best, but the ordeal challenged Jeff's spiritual life as he remained unemployed for over a year.

People's Viewpoint

There are a number of ways people could have responded

to Jeff's situation. The response of the company that laid him off might have been cold and matter of fact. I am sure some of Jeff's coworkers had their views. Some probably expressed empathy while others remained silent, not able to sort out their own despair. How did the Christians around him respond? Some might have acknowledged the difficulties by showing their concern and understanding while others could have tried to help Jeff by giving their spiritual interpretation for the dire circumstances. These explanations often come from different angles and points of views. One view might focus on Satan's desire to devour Jeff by eliminating his job. Another might view Jeff's job loss as a chastisement from God for some wrong doing. Some might even think that Jeff lost his job due to the fact that he did not pray enough or give enough tithes to God. Then, others might think that Jeff would never have lost his job if he just had enough faith in God to deliver him.

All of these views have an element of truth to them, but each one by itself lacks correlation with the rest of Scripture. They all take a truth out of the Bible and try to apply it to Jeff's situation wanting to explain why God allowed this to happen. *Using Scripture in such a way can be confusing and hurtful to those at whom it is aimed.*

Often our natural tendency is to try to explain God's reasoning. We should not feel it is our duty to somehow cover for God when actually we don't know why He has chosen to allow certain things to happen. Generally speaking, God has not called His people to try to figure out His ways on matters they cannot understand.[1] However, what God has revealed to us in His written Word is said to be sufficient and essential for living in every circumstance.[2]

What Is Good - What Is Better

Why is it that God did not make life to just be easy and full of pleasures? Wouldn't that be His best interest for me? Doesn't He realize how much better my life would be if I did not have all these problems at work and home? It's precisely with these questions that we have our greatest struggles. We expect that if God fulfilled our dreams by giving us a lifelong job with a lush retirement, we'd be guaranteed a life of quality, enhancing our charitable capacity. Then, when these things don't come to fruition we ponder why our view of "good" is so much different from God's. All this points to the fact that there is a vast difference between what the world tells us is "the good life" and God's way to the "better life".

Some Christians would lead us to believe that God's ultimate purpose for blessing us is to grant a life of maximum comfort, pleasure, and good health. It is no wonder why people who believe this become disillusioned with God when things don't turn out the way they had expected.

How is it that we fault God for failing to accomplish what we think is good when He has a plan for something better? For example, my reasoning might be that if everything in my life would run smoothly with no frustrations and problems, my life would be perfect. God knows it is better for me to go through periods of testing and trials so that I learn patience, diligence, and contentment. There is no doubt that God finds pleasure in giving us good things to enjoy and to delight us.[3] It is equally true that God often allows us to face trials and adversities for growing our faith which would never be accomplished by just living "the good life."[4]

God's higher goal for us conflicts with the world's impaired view of living a life of ease. This does not mean that God wants to fill our lives with misery and sadness. He does not! He allows things like sorrow, loss, and adversity to develop His qualities in us. These lead us to experience His presence in all circumstances of life in a deeper and better way. Of course this means that we put our trust in Him by our willingness to yield to His guidance along the way.

God promises us that the end results of our trials will someday far outweigh the present temporary hardships.[5] His interest involves the process of transforming us - not an immediate transformation - but a lasting one. As we learn to rely on God and trust His Word in our trials, He has promised to mature, strengthen, and firmly establish us through them.[6] No company or job could deliver this promise to us. No salary, bonus, or retirement could give us the kind of security and peace the way God can. *Simply put "the better life" comes from the hand of God, which money cannot buy, promotions cannot achieve, and pleasure cannot deliver.* Rather it is a quality of life which is being formed in us as we learn to trust and obey the Lord in the midst of life's challenges. Jeff learned this, and his life is enriched because of it. You should meet Jeff today! He did get another job with greater responsibilities and more opportunities to trust God and watch Him work in new ways.

More Than A Simulated Experience

Let's face it...technology fascinates and captivates us! We can participate in computer games which give us the sensation that we are involved in real-life activities and surroundings. Although we call them virtual reality, they are only "make believe". Just imagine! You've entered an airplane and discover the pilots have hundreds of hours of flight time...but only in a simulator. In other words, the pilots have never flown in real conditions. You would probably feel somewhat uneasy and question whether or not you are willing to entrust your life into their hands. Ok, if you gave them the benefit of the doubt, they might do all right on takeoff and landing, but their orientation and flying skills still would not have been tested in real life and therefore their training is incomplete. A full-fledged pilot is one who has learned the skills and has been tested beyond the experience of a simulator with many flight hours in a real plane and in real flying conditions.

Often, we Christians exercise our faith in God exclusively within a controlled simulated experience. We attend Christian activities on a regular basis, where we are instructed in the essentials of the Christian faith and taught how to walk by faith. It is here that we are also trained in spiritual disciplines, possibly even acting them out in a skit or viewing them on video. It is not that the "simulated" experiences we learn at church or other Christian meetings are not important...they are very important! However, if our faith in the Lord is not exercised and tested out in the world, then it is not much more than "virtual reality." In God's bigger picture, we see how part of our faith is trained and grows as we gather in our churches. The other part develops as it is lived out and tested in the everyday circumstances out in the world.

When humanity decided not to follow God's ways, as recorded in Genesis 3, God subjected the world to conditions that would work against it. For instance, we know that the world is declining and wearing out, as both energy and matter are depleting. Humans apart from God are not evolving into better beings, for without God's help they are actually becoming more selfish and debase. God allowed these adverse conditions to remind us of our need for Him. At the same time He uses these conditions to train and mature His people by purifying and strengthening their faith. It was James who wrote, *"Consider it all joy, my brethren, when you encounter various trials, knowing that the testing of your faith produces endurance. And let endurance have its perfect result, so that you may be perfect and complete, lacking in nothing."* [7]

These conditions also provide an opportunity for us to experience God's faithfulness and love toward us. Having knowledge about God's faithfulness is one-dimensional, but seeing Him provide the needed resources to get us through difficulties gives us a fuller picture of His faithfulness. Also, we might accept God's forgiveness for ourselves, but we only gain its fuller meaning when we forgive those who have wronged us.

God is using the current conditions around us, including our workplace, to make us spiritually mature in Him. It is here where our understanding of God's Word and our trust in His character are tested and tried. Tough circumstances provide us the opportunity to know God in ways that we otherwise could not have known Him. The following story is one that illustrates this in a profound way and one that I witnessed personally.

Gary is a wonderful godly man who has been an airline pilot for years. He is a good friend and we have ministered to airlines people together. He has also served as one of our FCAP Board Members for a number of years. Gary has experienced spiritual success as he watched God work in unique and marvelous ways in his life. However, not in the way you might imagine. If you asked Gary how he has seen success within his airline career, he would probably show you five different airline uniforms in his closet. You see... his personal journey has led him through five airline bankruptcies. And yet, Gary would tell you that he would not be the man he is today without God allowing him to go through these adversities. Gary's experiences have also given him more opportunities for personal growth and ministry than he ever could have imagined. Listen to Gary's own words describing his journey.

> "Throughout the several ordeals, my faith was tested. There were times when I simply hung on by choice. There was little to no joy. There were only God's Word and His promises. I sometimes walked mechanically through these valleys, knowing the right

things to do, but down deep inside I could not reconcile the "why" of my several trying experiences, until much later. In spite of walking through about 12 years of abrasive days in the airlines, struggling to make sense of it, I just kept walking...far from perfectly, but I kept walking and seeking the Lord. It was anything but easy.

My message is this: At no time, although things got very tight, did I ever miss a meal that was not by choice. I always had a roof over my head. I had food in the cupboard, and the Lord opened numerous doors throughout the world where I had the privilege of ministering in more than a dozen countries.

At present, I have a good job in the aviation industry where I teach airline pilots from all over the world in state-of-the-art flight simulators. There is also the possibility that my current job may melt away, but I know that should this happen, I'm going to be OK. I've got 5 different uniforms in my closet that testify to His faithfulness. As I trained myself to look at HIM and not on the circumstance, I can look back and see how the Lord ALWAYS remained faithful, and took care of me. The other part of my message is that each of us MUST focus carefully and humbly on the Lord. He is our resource. He is our life! He will not let us down. If our focus is on our job, our 401K, the politicians in Washington, or whatever, we are indulging in the sin of idolatry. The sooner we get all of this straight, the sooner the Lord can entrust us with more of Himself and His resources."[8]

We are told that now we can only see the "big picture" dimly.[9] However, God wants to assure us that He will complete the good work that He has begun in us.[10] He might incorporate some of our goals and plans and He might allow some trials, but His goal in the process is to conform us into His image. Our ultimate satisfaction and fulfillment of life will not be found in our achievements or momentary pleasures but in knowing God deeply, trusting God fully, and submitting to God's transforming process in our lives.

DISCUSSION QUESTIONS

1. Reflect on Jeff's story...on how he lost his job and how he was humiliated. What would you have said to him to encourage him at the time?

2. Showing compassion toward people was one of Jesus Christ's main traits during his time on earth (Matthew 9:36). Name some ways you can show compassion toward coworkers with whom you have differences?

3. If God allows certain conditions in the workplace at times to challenge us in order to mature us, describe some of the conditions in your workplace which have challenged your faith.

4. Can you name one problem on the job you would like God to change or remove? If yes, what have you learned through this difficulty? How has it changed your thinking, attitude, and actions?

5. Difficulties are not enjoyable. However, God often uses them to turn us in a direction that is better for us and usually only realized in the long run. Looking back in your life, can you recall such incidences?

BEING
THE CHURCH
IN THE
WORKPLACE

WHEN

WHEN
GOD
SHOWS UP AT
WORK

10

MAKING OUR CONNECTIONS

Daniel worked in the computer division of his airline company. We had met periodically for lunch and talked about God and our workplace. I recall how at one of our lunch meetings he came looking somewhat down and a bit frustrated. I asked him if something was wrong. He said: "yes," and began telling about his recent conversations with three other Christians around him at work. I remember the illustration he used to describe how close they worked from each other. He said: "If I were to wad up a piece of paper into a ball, I could throw it and hit any one of them." They were all aware that each one was a Christian and they all attended a different local church. Daniel had approached them to ask if they would like to meet once a week for a few minutes during their lunch breaks to pray for one another, for the people around them, and for their company. He had several talks with them, but the group never formed. It seemed every time they started discussing the possibility it inevitably ended in an argument over their different views or whose church was better. I could see how this was a great disappointment to Daniel.

Sadly, many Christians go into the workplace feeling alone or maybe just wanting to be left alone. They don't see any reason to connect with other Christians, except for those obviously required by the nature of their work. According to

God's Word, Christians are said to be God's family, a part of His household, and yet the evidence of this in the workplace can be practically non-existent. During our training session when discussing the subject of this chapter, I often ask the group: "Would you say that the Christians in your workplace treat one another like family?" Most often the responses are no different than the responses Daniel received.

Why is this? Could it be that some Christians feel they don't have the time for this at work? This would be understandable. Maybe some just don't think it is important and cannot see what difference it would make... so why bother? Then there are Christians who do associate through company events and clubs. Though I would encourage Christians to be involved in these things, they really don't draw attention to the greater connection Christians have together in Christ. Maybe you feel somewhat like Daniel. You have interacted with other Christians at work, but the focus was on your differences rather than on what you spiritually share in common. Why can't we see the importance of our identifying with one another in the workplace?

Up to this point in the book, I have stressed the importance of seeing God in connection to your work and workplace in three primary ways. First, I talked about understanding God in relationship to your work by developing a God-sized view of work. Next, I described how God's ministry in the workplace is integrated in the details of your work. Then, I stressed the importance of responding to workplace conditions God's way. Now, I would like us to consider how God's people can connect in the workplace to bring the church's influence there. How important is this...and will it make a difference?

Being The Church - Not Just Going To Church

Our perception of "the church" can be quite restrictive when we only see it as a place we go to once or twice a week. Let me stress again that being involved in a local church is a very important part of your spiritual life. However, the church does not somehow dissolve or become lifeless when the local church meeting disbands.

The Bible describes the church in two forms.[1] One is the local church where Christians gather at a designated time and place to worship together, learn God's truths, and show mutual support in various ways. The other is the universal church or "Body of Christ"[2] which represents Christ's presence through His people throughout the world. The term Body of Christ is the most comprehensive expression of the church in the Bible. It depicts all believers in Christ, regardless of their languages, nationalities, and cultures as parts of one body under one head - Christ. Support and nourishment among the parts and growth of the body takes place as each part understands its connection to the Head (Christ) and how they function together with the other parts of the body.

God has chosen to live within His people and not in things made by humans. When Christ is present in our local churches, He is there primarily through His people in whom He lives.

> The God who made the world and all things in it, since He is Lord of heaven and earth, does not dwell in temples made with hands. (Acts 17:24)
>
> ...For we are the temple of the living God; just as God said, "I WILL DWELL IN THEM AND WALK AMONG THEM; AND I WILL BE THEIR GOD, AND THEY SHALL BE MY PEOPLE." (2 Corinthians 6:16)

The presence of the living God is the distinguishing mark of His people.[3] *God's people bring His presence to the workplace just as much as they bring it to church!*

Vital Signs of the Body

You may be thinking to yourself...I really don't see "the church" in my workplace...so what does it look like anyway? Because we have a living Lord who works through "His body", the church should be showing some vital signs. If you found a person laying on the ground unconscious what vital signs would you look for? First, you would look to see if the person was breathing while at the same time checking for a heart beat or pulse. These two signs are the most basic indicators to whether a person is alive and if his body is still functional. If the Body of Christ is said to represent the presence of the living God in the world and in our workplaces, there will be vital signs that indicate it is alive there.

Making Your Connection

In the second chapter of his epistle to the Ephesians, Paul draws attention to the importance of Christians demonstrating the connection they have in Christ. He starts by pointing out that all people regardless of their background share the same origin, that of being born in sin which separates them from God. God's personal invitation to be reconciled and enter His family is for all people, not just a certain group of people.

When Paul wrote these things, there were some Jewish believers who felt their faith in God was a little purer because of their background. But Paul declares in this passage that we were given a new identity; that our right to enter into God's family no longer depended on our background but rather on Christ's identity. Because of this, we have a new association to one another that transcends national, cultural, corporate, or even blood relationships.

During that time there was a growing tendency among

Christians to focus on and emphasize their differences, similar to what Daniel experienced with his three coworkers. Listen to how Paul defends his point by underscoring the importance of Christians connecting to one another.

He starts out by saying *Christians are no longer to act like strangers and aliens to one another* (2:19). At one time or another all of us have observed foreigners move to our homeland. They come bringing their different customs and ways of life. We sometimes tend to keep our distance and simply coexist with them. This defines the type of relationship Daniel felt he had with the three other Christian coworkers. They worked around one another, acknowledged their Christian faith, but by focusing on their differences, they merely coexisted at their workplace. Such behavior contradicts the redemptive work of Christ which broke down walls between us. The workplace will not benefit from the influence of the Body of Christ when Christians act like strangers to one another.

Paul goes on to strengthen his point by describing the kind of relationship Christians have to one another. Instead of seeing each other as strangers and aliens, *we should consider ourselves as fellow citizens*. Citizens are people who share the same rights, benefits, and protection under the laws of their country. In a similar way, all of God's people share in the same spiritual blessings, rights, and privileges. We have equal access to God and share in the same riches in Christ. Regardless of our nationality, language, and church affiliation we are fellow citizens of an eternal kingdom.[4]

Next, Paul personalizes our relationship to one another as Christians by stating *we are of Christ's household, the family of God*. The family unit in any culture provides the most intimate place for humans to relate to one another. We have our greatest opportunity to develop and mature in the family. My family knows me best and continues to love me despite my failures and weaknesses, showing me patience, and encouraging me to grow. When Christians go into the workplace, they not only bring their individual relationship with God, they bring God's familial relationship as well.[5]

For Christians to argue over issues like what church they go to, what mode of baptism they prefer, whether they are reformed, dispensational, charismatic, pre...post...or A-mil is not building relationships on the same foundation. We don't need to hide our differences so the world can't see them. We need to demonstrate that though we have differences they don't divide us. Why? Because the foundation of our family identity is Christ and His continuing work in and through us.

Paul's final point in Ephesians 2 speaks of the far reaching influence Christians possess.

> ...Having been built on the foundation of the apostles and prophets, Christ Jesus Himself being the corner *stone,* in whom the whole building, being fitted together, is growing into a holy temple in the Lord, in whom you also are being built together into a dwelling of God in the Spirit. (Ephesians 2:20-22)

Referring to the tabernacle and the temple in the Old Testament (which were designated places for God's presence to dwell), Paul depicts **Christians being fitted together as one body of people** for the purpose of growing into a holy temple...God's dwelling place. His analogy is pointed and profound!

When Christians act like family instead of strangers to one another, they become a habitation for God's presence. We know from Scripture that God's presence dwells in each of His children.[6] However, Paul is saying there is a special sense of God's presence, like that of the temple and tabernacle when

Christians connect as family. This is not limited to our local church meetings. *Whenever Christians demonstrate their togetherness, they become a place where God's presence is given greater exposure.*

In September of 2002, I was asked by the leaders of an FCAP group to participate with them in a 9/11 Memorial Service their pilot union was hosting. It was a wonderful occasion and very well attended. After the service several pilots came up to me to express their appreciation in my coming. I was struck by some of the comments a few of these pilots made. Three pilots separately conveyed to me that all of the pilots in their company knew about these Christian pilots. Though this FCAP group was not big, their connection and activities in the workplace brought awareness to all the pilots in their airline. Later I told Mike, our FCAP coordinator, that their connection as Christians was radiating obvious signs of a "living church" to all the pilots in their company.

Building Our Connections in the Workplace

When we talk about "making our connection" it is not something we create. Christians are connected together in Christ because of what God has done. We cannot do anything to become more connected, but we are to develop this connection. We are told in the Bible to make every effort to keep the unity of spirit in the bond of peace.[7] Christ is our connection, but now we need to develop and maintain it among us. Let's look at some ways to develop our connection in the workplace.

When constructing a building we must first start by laying its foundation. The foundation provides alignment and support for the structure.[8] So it is with Christians connecting together at the workplace. We must begin to align our relationships with one another on the same foundation, Jesus Christ. This means we should start by considering together our individual relationships with Christ. Marc, our FCAP coordinator in Zurich, once told me that when new people came to their FCAP meetings he would not ask them where they go to church. Instead he started by finding out about their relationship and walk with Christ. A good topic for a group discussion among Christians would be to consider, "How does my personal relationship with Christ affect my work and my relationships at work?" We can reverse this question by asking, "How does my work affect my relationship with Christ?" Such exchanges will help Christians align their personal faith with one another and develop their connection.

The connection between Christians in the workplace can strengthen as we learn to share together God's truth and guidance from His Word. There simply is not enough time at work to argue over minor points and controversial topics of the Bible. So, we must focus on the main points of our faith and stay away from the minor ones. My two good friends, Scott and Tim, have become skilled in starting and maintaining groups in the workplace for almost two decades. They encourage Christians to stay away from discussing or arguing over matters that can easily and typically bring divisions among Christians.[9] Many of these things ultimately don't matter, especially in the workplace; they are divisive and push us off our common foundation in Christ. *It is always best to focus on the clear and direct teachings of Scripture that can be applied to our workplace environment and to our walk with Christ there.*

The connection Christians have in the workplace should reflect Christ's interest and focus less on our own agenda. What do people observe when they see Christians united in their workplace? Can they detect Christ has genuine concern and compassion for them? Coworkers who watch Christians gather solely to demonstrate their joint dislike over an issue will not see Christ, nor will they see Christ when Christians unite only for their own personal interests.

In the mid 1990's, I was in close contact with a few people who had organized a large gathering of Christians to pray for resolution of a pending strike which was affecting their company. They met and prayed several times during a few weeks and the meetings grew to several hundred. I thought it was a commendable and worthy cause. However, when it looked like the strike would be resolved, I suggested to the leaders they raise the group's interest to a higher level. I recommended they ask the whole group to consider continuing their weekly prayer meeting to seek and advance Christ's interest in their workplace. They announced this to everyone at the prayer meeting that week. The next week the negotiations were successful and things were back to normal... and the number of people attending the prayer meeting? They could be counted on one hand!

The authenticity of Christians connecting together will be evident when we connect for Christ's greater purposes. It should be obvious to the people who watch us that this is the compelling force in our lives in every circumstance.

An essential vital sign which could serve as a summary to what we've looked at thus far is how Christian's demonstrate their love for each another. Christ stakes His reputation before the world by the love that is demonstrated among Christians. When this love is exhibited, Jesus said, "the world will know you are my own."[10]

Taking Faith Steps

We are told that *"without faith it is impossible to please Him (God), for he who comes to God must believe that He is and that He is a rewarder of those who seek Him."*[11] Exercising faith in God means I am trusting God to work through me.

Oftentimes my taking faith steps provide opportunities for me to see God in a bigger way and experience His resources more personally. Making our connection in the workplace requires us to take such steps of faith there.

There are a few basic faith steps you can take to connect with other Christians in the workplace. Begin by praying for the people and circumstances around you while also praying for God's guidance. Next, you should take a step of faith and begin seeking out and identifying other Christians around you. I used to think that most people knew this and that this step sounded too obvious and simple. But this simple step has brought about some wonderful stories in people's lives who attended our trainings. One of these was from a lady who worked in the reservations center of her airline. At the end of our training she shared how much the session on the importance of praying for the people and situations in the workplace impressed her. She also told the group how for the first time she had become aware of the church being a living presence and influence at the workplace. She shared how inspired she was to go back to work and put these steps into practice. Here is part of her first email to us after she had gone back to work:

> I have exciting news; my discussion with my lead (supervisor) regarding workplace ministry went very well. He promised his support and immediately sent emails to the department manager and center director... I have seven confirmed interested people...this is all happening much faster than I thought.[12]

The connection God's people make in the workplace ministry can occur in a number of creative ways. It is not about following a certain paradigm, using clever techniques, or gathering the right number of people in the right place. It is about people, who, in the ordinary settings of work, believe that God can work through them to bring His presence to their coworkers. Here is another amazing example of this through a man named Bob.

Bob came to one of our FCAP trainings because the local church he attended hosted one. His pastor, Pete, was bivocational working also as an airline mechanic. At his airline job, Pete was part of an FCAP group that met over lunch breaks. He decided to host the FCAP training at his church and extended an invitation to anyone working in or outside the airline industry. Bob worked in a management position at a food processing plant with several hundred employees. As the training progressed, Bob's eyes were opened to things that he had not considered about his workplace. By the end of the training, he knew what steps of faith he wanted to take considering his time limitations at work. He told us he only had ten, maybe fifteen minutes available during a break time, but he was willing to start there and see what God would do. One week later Bob called to tell me that he had two others who were interested in meeting for prayer during their 10-minute break once a week. I could hear the excitement in his voice. Two weeks passed then Bob called again. Enthusiastically, he told me that some others had joined and now there were eight at the weekly meeting. I received his third call a couple weeks later asking if I could meet him for lunch. He went on to explain the reason for the lunch meeting; the General Manager of the plant wanted to meet me. At that lunch meeting Bob introduced me to Phil, the Plant Manager. I learned quickly that Phil was a Christian. He wanted to thank me personally for teaching this training because he could see the transformation take place with only a few Christians in his plant. He went on to explain that for years he watched Christians draw attention to special events or issues that were important to them, but he had never seen a group of Christians take such genuine interest in the people and circumstances at their workplace like this group. Phil was so encouraged and impressed that he wanted to be part of it though he needed to be cautious due to his position. Bob told of the variety of prayers the group was praying for; personal needs, machines breaking down, challenging relationships within the company and many others. He wanted the other several hundred employees in the plant to feel a part of their prayer meeting, realizing that most of these employees probably couldn't attend due to the different break times. He decided to send out a company memo letting employees know that they could drop off their prayer requests. He dedicated one of the big whiteboards in his office and invited any employee to come at anytime and write his or her request on it. As time went on, the board was filled with more and more requests, most of which centered on situations at the plant and personal needs.

I met with Bob and Phil again and they had further news to tell me. There were now two prayer groups that were meeting weekly, one in the evening and the other in the morning. Phil shared that he shows up unannounced at the prayer meetings when his schedule allows. Then Bob informed me that he was beginning to make contact with some employees at another plant whom he thought would be interested in forming prayer groups. Just think, in the beginning all Bob knew he had were ten to fifteen minutes during his break time, but he was willing to take steps of faith and trust God to do the rest. Do you see any possibilities around you at work? Are you willing to take steps of faith that require you to trust God to work through you? I commend the courageous faith of the men and women who have been used to connect Christians together in the workplace. Their worthy efforts may not be fully realized, but the results are more than the eye can see and someday they will be fully rewarded.

My prayer is - **May their numbers increase!**

DISCUSSION QUESTIONS

1. Would you say that the Christians at your workplace treat each other as family?
2. Name some characteristics among Christians in the workplace that would indicate to those around them that they are like family.
3. If having a balanced understanding between the local church and universal church is essential, how could embracing only one while neglecting the other affect us in a negative way?
4. Do you see God getting greater exposure at work by the way Christians treat each other like family? How does this impact the work environment?
5. Some Christians from different churches form a group in their workplace. Name some core truths from God's word that would be essential in their maintaining unity and keeping their focus on a mutual purpose while in the workplace. Also, name some teachings that should not be majored on, in order to avoid divisions?
6. When talking about building our connections with other believers at our workplace, what faith steps could you take to connect Christians in your workplace? Lay out some practical steps you could prayerfully take.

—— 11 ——

THE CHURCH
ON THE MOVE

I was 26 years old when I went to Europe for the first time to study at L'Abri Fellowship in a small village up in the Swiss Alps. The whole experience broadened my horizons. So many impressions from that time still influence my life today. One of those many experiences was seeing and hearing the history of some ancient European landmarks of the Christian faith. I enjoyed very much visiting some of the old churches that still resonate with their old pipe organs and exhibit the eloquent architecture of towering steeples, stained glass windows, and works of art. Such impressive buildings! However, many of these landmarks are more like museums today. They are scarcely used by a few people for the purpose for which they were built.

When I reflect on Christ's words in Matthew 16:18, I ask myself what Jesus meant when He said, "**I will build my church.**" Did He mean beautiful buildings? Maybe, but not likely! Certainly equating Christ's purpose of building His church to the construction of beautiful buildings is not an adequate explanation; especially since there is no record of a church building until the latter part of the third century AD. Prior to that time, the church for the most part met in homes and in some public places. So, what exactly did Christ have in mind when he told His disciples, "I will build my church and the gates of

Hades will not prevail against it"? Did Christ have some kind of blue-print and certain measurements in determining how He would build His church?

History bears witness to the fact that the Christian church has been a moving force within most western cultures. Under its influence came the forming of government, education, schools, hospitals, orphanages, and many other institutions. If these cultures had not held the core beliefs and values of the Christian faith, they would not have created such institutions. But history also shows that when the church became more of a politically motivated institution, its spiritual influence diminished.

With today's globalization, governments are now emphasizing pluralism and secular communities. This movement views the Christian church as a hindrance to its progress. Christians, especially in western cultures, feel they have lost ground and are having to redefine their relationship to a growing post Christian and postmodern world. The church in most cultures is now considered to be on the outer edges of culture with a marginal influence at best. If most cultures no longer recognize the church as a part of society, than how is Christ building His church in today's world? What should it look like? How will it involve me? And how should it affect my workplace?

I believe the words of Jesus Christ as found in Matthew 16:13-18 provide us the starting point of how Christ continues to build His Church.

> Now when Jesus came into the district of Caesarea Philippi, He was asking His disciples, "Who do people say that the Son of Man is?" And they said, "Some *say* John the Baptist; and others, Elijah; but still others, Jeremiah, or one of the prophets." He said to them, "But who do you say that I am?" Simon

> Peter answered, "You are the Christ, the Son of the living God." And Jesus said to him, "Blessed are you, Simon Barjona, because flesh and blood did not reveal *this* to you, but My Father who is in heaven. I also say to you that you are Peter, and upon this rock I will build My church; and the gates of Hades will not overpower it. (Matthew 16:13-18)

Understanding this will help us to better see how Christ is working through his people in today's world and workplaces to build His church.

The Big Question

The setting of the Matthew passage gives us an insightful angle which we cannot afford to miss. Jesus was walking through the region of Caesarea Philippi with His disciples. *"Perhaps while looking at the various shrines built on the nearby hillside to honor man-made gods, Jesus began to talk about public opinion."*[1] The gods in those days were often central to the culture and shaped people's beliefs about life. These gods were greatly esteemed and considered the celebrities of their day. I can imagine Jesus walking through the countryside looking at all this, engaging with his disciples, asking them why people viewed these gods as symbols of greatness.

Jesus then presents them with the first loaded question: *"Who do people say that I am?"* Of course Christ knew what people thought about Him, but He wanted to address public opinion with His disciples. Their comments were revealing. *"Some say John the Baptist; and others, Elijah; but still others, Jeremiah, or one of the prophets."*[2] Their answers confirmed that popular opinion was willing to acknowledge that Jesus might be some resurrected hero. However, they missed His true identity...that of being the Creator and Lord of the universe. In a similar way, people today have no problem seeing Jesus as some cosmic angel who does extraordinary things to inspire people. This idea about Jesus is no threat to them and it coincides with the current sensationalism of the day; but to talk about Jesus Christ as Savior and Lord? Popular opinion would consider this is going too far because to believe this would require them to be accountable.

The very next question Jesus asked was meant to be personal and direct. A good question does more than test our knowledge about facts, it reveals our personal views and decisions in light of the facts! If you asked my wife, Claudette, "Who do people say Paul Curtas is?" Her answer would not necessarily be personal. She would probably convey common known facts about me, my education, my current job title, or my current place of employment. But if you posed the question, "Who do you say Paul is?" Her response would be personal and reveal the relationship we have to each other. Jesus' question did just that; it was aimed at revealing the disciples' relationship with Him!

I can only imagine the scene when Christ was about to ask this second question. He may have looked away from them to gaze into the distance for a moment as he began the question, *"By the way"*... then turning His head, looking directly into their eyes... *"...Who do you say that I am?"*[3] We don't know if there was a time of silence or not. I wouldn't be surprised to find out there was. But eventually Peter blurts out: *"You are the Christ, the Son of the living God!"* Jesus made sure they knew there is a great blessing in knowing and believing this truth. However, He also needed to clarify that Peter did not come up with this on his own initiative. This truth had been revealed to him and eventually it would be revealed to the other disciples and they would be used by God to make it known to people throughout the world.

Peter's declaration of Christ being Lord is foundational to how the church is being built. Jesus said: *"Upon this rock...* Christ's Lordship...*I will build my church."*[4] Rock was important building material in that day since buildings in that region were often made of rock and started with a rock called the cornerstone. The Scriptures declare that Christ is the cornerstone,[5] and that there is no other foundation to build life upon other than Him. *"For no man can lay a foundation other than the one which is laid, which is Jesus Christ."*[6] Christ does not use rock, stone, and mortar to build His church. He is building it by establishing authentic personal relationships with people and fitting them together as His body of people. The saving work and Lordship of Christ, the rock, provides a stable foundation and support through life.[7] When Jesus Christ declares He is building His church, He is doing so as individual people receive Him as their Savior and Lord.

But this is not only a personal matter; it is a global one as well. Christ has infiltrated more cultures of the world than any other faith or political ideology. People from diverse cultures have been presented with Jesus and received Him as their Savior and Lord. The effect of Christ's work in people's lives is the same regardless of their backgrounds and vast differences. They are known by His distinctive marks.[8]

When the disciples saw Christ resurrected from the dead, they fully understood and made known His identity. News about Jesus spread rapidly as people were being confronted with who He was. The apostle Paul and other disciples traveled the Roman Empire reasoning with people of all positions about the uniqueness of Jesus Christ.[9] Peter made an appeal to people by asking them to consider "this Jesus." [10] CS Lewis, the renowned Cambridge Scholar and author of *The Chronicles of Narnia,* came to a deciding point in his life when his good friend, JRR Tolkien, challenged him to consider who Jesus really is ...*the Lord God...or a liar and a lunatic!*

You will find that people can easily discuss and argue over seeming discrepancies in the Bible or what they think are outdated traditions. But ask them what they think about Jesus Christ and who He really is and it can make them uncomfortable. Some may even feel it is too personal of a question...and it is...very personal! Because Jesus Christ is building His church by people personally being confronted with who He is and what they believe in light of Him.

Pointing the Way - Not Making Your Point

Christ continues to build His church today by using His people to convey the same question He asked His disciples. We are said to be God's personal invitation to people and He is making His appeal to the world through us; "*Therefore, we are ambassadors for Christ, as though God were making an appeal through us.*"[11] We participate in His building the church as we uniquely present Christ to people around us. There are two basic ways we bring Jesus' identity to people. We can use words to tell about Him or our lives can demonstrate His Lordship through our actions. One way is not better than the other and each complements the other.[12]

When an opportunity opens up to share the Gospel with words, it is important we do so because the content of the Gospel message is endowed with the power of God, which leads a person to salvation.[13] We can also use words to point people to Christ by sharing what He means to us personally or by asking them a question that would invite them to consider Christ. However, remember your effectiveness is not based on how well you can argue for Christ and how loud or boldly you can state your case, but how well you point the way. Just stating our points requires no personal interaction with people. Christ never intended to send us out to act like a video recording to people. If He wanted that He could have written His message on stones or in the sky or have the birds sing it.

Another way people will consider Christ is by the way we demonstrate His Lordship in our lives. Just as God has endowed the Gospel message with power, He endows His witnesses with power and influence. People will observe our faith in God by the way we do our work and the way we treat people. Our conduct can also trigger the right kind of questions about God in people's minds. Showing exceptional grace and kindness to our coworkers can make them curious about the reason for our actions. People can also become inquisitive when they see that we don't do certain things others are doing like complaining or cheating. Whether we realize it or not, our actions provide a road sign that could eventually point people to Christ. The compelling influence the Lordship of Christ has on our lives in the workplace is of equal importance to talking about Him there. Our lives should be a personal invitation to observe a life that is built on the Rock...Christ.

At our FCAP India Convention in 2009, four people shared how they came to know Christ personally. Two of them told how they were introduced to Christ. They indicated that they would have never gone to a Christian church because of their own religious background. However, both of them were introduced to Christ by watching a couple of coworkers living out their Christian faith. This exposure eventually led them to talk with their Christian coworkers and consider Jesus Christ. The opportunity people have to see a living relationship with Jesus Christ through Christians is equally important to how well Christians can articulate the message with words.

When people show us their skepticism about Christ, we

must be careful not to become frustrated with their ideas and comments or push them to change their views. Even those who walked daily with Jesus on earth expressed disbelief and doubts about His identity.[14] Jesus gave people the opportunity to ponder and even struggle over the question of who He was. He was not forceful or condescending to them. Instead He showed patience and gentleness as he welcomed their questions and comments. As His authentic witnesses... how do we handle such incidents? How do we treat those who disbelieve, disagree, even poke fun and ridicule us?

Tim is a good friend of mine and a FCAP Board Member. He told me a story about a fellow worker (let's call him Don) who approached him at work. A bit sarcastically Don asked Tim to show him a miracle right on the spot or tell him of one he had recently witnessed. Tim's answer caught Don off guard. Gently laying his hand on Don's shoulder, Tim responded that he could give evidence of a miracle right then. He said: "Considering the kind of person I once was and the fact that I am now able to have genuine love for you is nothing less than a miracle." How do people perceive Christ through us? Is their perception of Him dimmed by our coldness, impatience, or maybe even our disdain of them? Or do they see Christ by how we welcome their questions and listen to their ideas and beliefs, while at the same time showing them the love and mercy of Christ?

Our Penetrating Influence

There is one more important aspect to consider from the Matthew 16 passage about how Christ is building His church today and how it is on the move in our workplace. In order to build His church, Christ has determined to make his Lordship known by sending His people out among the shadow of the gates of Hades. He is building it by moving His people out into their everyday routines of life, where they encounter opposition, conflict, chaos, and they intersect with people that are very different. Christ has put us on the offensive, in order to move us out among people in the shadows of the gates of Hades.

A person on the offensive is characterized by his moving into an opponent's territory or an enemy's stronghold. On the other hand, a person on the defensive is in a fixed location where he constructs a fortress in order to protect and control his influence and authority. The imagery Jesus uses in this passage to make His point is powerful. The gates[15] of Hades depict Satan's fortification by which he binds people with his stronghold. We are told he uses lies, deception, fear, and hatred to destroy what is sound and wholesome. His authority increases as people give in to his ways. You have probably seen this develop in the workplace. A work environment becomes oppressive or depressive as it is taken over by anger or fear.

The picture here is Christ building His church by moving the people of God into territories where Satan is trying to build his fortification by binding people to his ways. Though we cannot see them with our physical eyes, we do see the effects of Satan's influence and its strongholds on people personally and collectively. Yet when God's people approach these fortifications, walking obediently under Christ's Lordship, they bring with them the power of God's presence like a battering ram upon their gates.

Christ is not asking us to study the traits of evil people or focus on Satan and his tactics.[16] Christ is asking that we walk obediently by faith under His Lordship. This will determine our effectiveness among the shadow of the gates of Hades. Christ is building His church by moving the people of God out among people who are trapped in darkness and need His great light. Christ describes these people like sheep without a shepherd who are being harassed and oppressed by the darkness.[17]

When our lives intersect with these needy people it can

become uncomfortable for them and us. They can feel exposed by the light and react to it, while we can feel vulnerable among the strongholds of darkness. Such confrontation will challenge our weaknesses and stretch our faith in God. Yet this is how Christ is building His church. He is sending us out into our world and our workplaces everyday to radiate His light among those in darkness.

Though many cultures of the world may consider the church as marginal, Christ is still building His church by sending His people among them. I am concerned with the diminishing influence Christians are having within their cultures and in their workplaces. As the world is changing and increasingly opposing Christ, it seems that Christians are retreating more and more within the walls of their church in order to protect and reassure their faith. The local church plays a vital role in Christ building His church. It offers an environment and structure that is needed for Christians to learn truth and worship God. However, if the church's influence resides mostly within its walls, should we be surprised that the culture around it is deteriorating? The most important influence on any civilization, any culture, or any company is God's presence actively working through His people.

The influence Christ exhibits through Christians in the workplace today embodies Him building His church. Though God reveals Himself through other means, He has chosen to manifest His presence through His people. **When God shows up at our workplace,** He will be working through His people to bring the knowledge of Christ there.

> But thanks be to God, who always leads us in triumph in Christ, and manifests through us the sweet aroma of knowledge of Him in everyplace.
> (2 Corinthians 2:14)

The contrast between the amount of time spent in the workplace in comparison to the amount of time spent at your church is staggering. You will have spent an estimated 90,000 hours in the workplace compared to 5,000 hours in church by the time you reach retirement. These 90,000 hours in the workplace not only represent a span of time spent there; they also represent a volume of time God could have used to display His presence through you.

Someday, would you want to look back with great joy knowing God worked through you at your workplace? Then remember this...

When God shows up at work... it will be through Christians who are doing their job for a God-sized reason and not merely for the company.

When God shows up at work... it will be through Christians who view the people and circumstances in their workplace as unique ministry opportunities from the Lord.

When God shows up at work... it will be through Christians who respond to the difficult people and situations of the workplace in God's way.

When God shows up at work... it will be through Christians who connect together demonstrating that the church is alive in the workplace.

When God shows up at work... you and your workplace will never be the same!

DISCUSSION QUESTIONS

1. What is the first thing you envision when you hear the word "church"?

2. Have you thought about what Christ meant when He said "*I will build my church*" and how have you understood that?

3. If Christ wants to use you to build His church in the workplace, give some examples how you can be involved as part of Him building it there.

4. Knowing that Christ is building His church by sending you out to interact with people who are overcome with darkness, how should you prepare yourselves to meet this challenge?

5. Describe some ways you can point your coworkers to Christ without using words.

6. Name some suggestions you could offer, or things you could do, to help your local church identify more with your ministry in the workplace.

APPENDIX

How Can I Know God?

How can I know God? This is a question many people ask themselves. The question is not just asked by teachers, philosophers, or preachers. It often arises from within, because we are created in the image of our Creator. Have you ever wondered who created the world and the universe and for what purpose? And if there is a creator, can I know Him personally?

People try to find the answer to this question in different ways. Some look at the universe for the answer. However, its greatness and complexity can be overwhelming. We can feel like a speck of dust in a huge cosmic mechanism. Though there is beauty and consistency to the universe, its greatness seems impersonal. Some look at the earth and nature to find answers. We see beauty in our world, but also we see disorder and cruelty. We hear the news about earthquakes, droughts, and tsunamis. Seeing natural disasters and their devastation makes us wonder why they happen and if anything can be done to stop them. Others may look at humanity and civilization to find answers, but these seem just as complex. We wonder why humans can be kind to one another and then again so cruel and hateful. This problem touches our own lives and we feel the effects of it personally. Many look for answers by searching for meaning in various religions, philosophies, and worldviews of which all have different founders and leaders.

If we look to the Bible, starting with the opening chapters of the book of Genesis, we find God's record of how He created the universe, the earth, and animals. It also describes a special creation of two creatures that would bear the Creator's image. These two people, named Adam and Eve, were given a place to live with responsibility and accountability to their Creator God. He gave them free range to work the garden and eat of most everything. He only asked that they trust Him by not eating the fruit of a certain tree. This tree was not evil in itself, but God chose to use it to test this man and woman's trust and reliance in their Creator. It wasn't long before they were tempted by a creature named Satan. He took advantage of their questions about God's restriction, leading them to desire to be like God, by ultimately becoming independent of Him.

Being deceived, they decided to eat of the tree that God told them not to eat. The result of their choice was catastrophic. It caused death over the whole creation. First, they personally felt guilty because it brought a separation between God and them. Their own bodies would now be subject to death and the dying process. Next, it brought resistance and even ruin to the human environment. Humans would from that time forward feel pain in their labor and in childbirth. Their relationships would be flawed by exploiting and manipulating one another. These and other affects would be ongoing and serve as a reminder, to everyone thereafter, that there is a basic problem known as sin in our world and in humans. Daily, humans face the consequences of the brokenness of life by choosing to do their own thing without God.

Thankfully, God did more than pronounce judgment on mankind. He proclaimed and provided the solution to bring restoration between the people and Himself. He began to reveal in various ways how He would ultimately provide the solution for us. However, the climax came when God himself entered history through the person of Jesus Christ, God's Son.

God, after He spoke long ago to the fathers in the

prophets in many portions and in many ways, in
these last days has spoken to us in His Son, whom
He appointed heir of all things, through whom also
He made the world. And He is the radiance of His
glory and the exact representation of His nature...
(Hebrews 1:1-3)

He came to earth in a humble way, being born as a baby,
growing up, and revealing His identity. He proclaimed that God,
His Father, gave Him as a ransom putting Him to death as an
innocent person at the hands of guilty people. Jesus Christ's
death on the cross was a public display of God's love for us, by
Him becoming our substitute and taking our judgment upon
Himself. *"He (God) made Him (Christ) who knew no sin to be
sin on our behalf, so that we might become the righteousness of
God in Him"* (2 Corinthians 5:21). God's love wasn't mere
words, nor was it cheap. His holy and perfect character required
Him to demonstrate that His dealing with sin and evil was done
justly and yet also mercifully. The cross of Christ met the
demands of justice as a ransom, while at the same time offered
forgiveness and new life.

...Being justified as a gift by His grace through the
redemption which is in Christ Jesus; whom God
displayed publicly as a propitiation in His blood
through faith. *This was* to demonstrate His
righteousness, because in the forbearance of God He
passed over the sins previously committed; for the
demonstration, *I say,* of His righteousness at the
present time, so that He would be just and the
justifier of the one who has faith in Jesus. (Romans
3:25-26).

His triumph over death was witnessed by many when He was resurrected from the dead three days after he was crucified, validating His claims to be God and fulfilling His mission to come as Savior of the world.

> For I delivered to you as of first importance what I also received, that Christ died for our sins according to the Scriptures, and that He was buried, and that He was raised on the third day according to the Scriptures, and that He appeared to Cephas, then to the twelve. After that He appeared to more than five hundred brethren at one time, most of whom remain until now... (1 Corinthians 15:3-8)

God's offer of salvation and new life is not based on race, nationality, social, or economic status. It is offered to all people, and it is offered freely, because the saving work is accomplished only through God's provision. We can do nothing to earn or achieve it on our own. Originally man and woman stepped away from God in order to become independent of Him. *In contrast, God's salvation is our taking a step toward becoming completely dependent on Him and His provision of salvation.* It can only be received as a gift because all of this is God's work. We receive this gift by faith, as a beggar would, with empty and open hands. By rejecting God's provision, we choose eternal separation from Him.

God's salvation promises us eternal life. But eternal life is more than you reaching a destination someday. It is about entering into a relationship with God right now where you are, regardless of the condition you are in. There are no degrees or levels we must reach in order to become savable by God. His salvation was accomplished and completed once and for all through Christ.

...We have been sanctified through the offering of the body of Jesus Christ once for all. For by one offering He has perfected for all time those who are sanctified. (Hebrews 10:10, 14)

Eternal life begins now by experiencing His forgiveness and His saving work in your life. *"This is eternal life, that they may know You, the only true God, and Jesus Christ whom You have sent."* (John 17:3)

Do you know God? Not just know about Him, but do you know Him personally? If not, His invitation is open to you:

- First recognize that God took the initiative to demonstrate His love by first loving us (John 3:16).
- Next, humbly admit to God your fallen condition without Him, and your own self-made independence from Him, and your total inability to help yourself.
- Then by faith...accept God's provision of salvation from your sins by trusting Christ and His redemptive work on the cross. We are told in the Bible that God's provision of salvation can only be received by faith. So, like a beggar with empty and open hands, receive God's forgiveness and new life today.

But as many as receive Him (Christ) to those who believe on His name, to them He gave the right to become children of God. (John 1:12)

END NOTES

Chapter 1: God-Sized View of Work

1. Miller, Keith – *The Taste of New Wine* – Author House 2009, Bloomington, IN; p.69
2. Genesis 2:15
3. Judith Allen Shelly; *Not Just a Job* (Intervarsity Press 1985) p15
4. Psalm 104:14
5. Judith Allen Shelly; *Not Just a Job* (Intervarsity Press 1985) p18
6. Colossians 3:23-24; Ephesians 6:7
7. The FCAP MSP Christmas Luncheon Dec 2, 1996
8. The Bible tells us that each person should determine in his or her own heart what amount they can cheerfully give and should not be coerced (2 Corinthians 9:7)

Chapter 2: The Root of Work- Past & Present

1. We are told in Genesis 2:2-3, when God finished his work He rested from work.
2. Nancy Pearcey, *Total Truth*, (Wheaton, Crossway Books 2004), p.48
3. Nancy Pearcey, *Total Truth*, (Wheaton, Crossway Books 2004), p.50
4. The apostle Paul described the distortion of sin in Romans 1:21-28; then in chapter 8:18-20 he tells how the whole of creation is groaning and waiting to be set free from the slavery of corruption.
5. It is both intensive - meaning we are capable of doing most any evil, and it is extensive - meaning every part of our makeup, our mind, will and emotions, has been affected by sin in some way or another.
6. Nancy Pearcey, *Total Truth*, (Wheaton, Crossway Books 2004), p.48
7. William Barclay, *Ethics in a Permissive Society*, (New York: Harper and Row 1971), p.94
8. William Barclay, *Ethics in a Permissive Society*, (New York: Harper and Row 1971), p.94.
9. Chuck Colson, Jack Eckert, *Why America Doesn't Work* (Dallas: Word Publishing, 1991), p.33
10. Chuck Colson, Jack Eckert, *Why America Doesn't Work* (Dallas: Word Publishing, 1991), p.33
11. Alvin J Schmidt, *Under the Influence* (Grand Rapids: Zondervan, 2001), p.194.

12. Matthew 20:26-28; 23:11
13. From the following two sources: The Expositors Bible Commentary (Grand Rapids: Zondervan, 1984); Volume 8; Mark: Walter W Wessel; p. 622. Also, Kenneth S Wuest; Word Studies in the Greek New Testament; (Grand Rapids: Eerdmans, 1974) Volume 1; pp.23-24;
14. Jim Rose, *Keynote Speaker at FCAP Convention, 1999*
15. Alvin J Schmidt, *Under the Influence,* (Grand Rapids: Zondervan, 2001), p.196.
16. For a more thorough study of this subject refer to John Murray, *Principles of Conduct,* (Grand Rapids, Eerdmans Publishing Co. 1981) pp.82-106 (Chapter 5- The Ordinance of Labor)
17. 2 Thessalonians 3:10
18. Mark A. Noll, *The Work We have to Do,* (New York: Oxford University Press 2002), p.20
19. William Tyndale, *Parable of the Wicked Mammon* (Toronto: Knox and Knox 1961), p.140.
20. 1 Corinthians 10:31
21. Chuck Colson, Jack Eckert, *Why America Doesn't Work,* (Dallas: Word Publishing, 1991), p. 39

Chapter 3: Expectations Influence Work

1. 1 Timothy 6:10; Hebrews 13:5
2. Ecclesiastes 5:12
3. Ecclesiastes 4:6
4. Ecclesiastes 5:19
5. Ecclesiastes 5:20
6. Matthew 6:30-34; Hebrews 13:5
7. Meaning the company will be healthy in many ways regardless of the size of profit.
8. Hebrews 13:5
9. Jeremiah 17:8
10. Jeremiah 17:6
11. This practice is especially valuable when a company is going through hard times.
12. Certainly I believe God could use such an occasion to lead you into a different job. Seek godly advice and allow God to make that clear to you, as you trust Him in your present circumstances.
13. 1Peter 2:18-21
14. 2 Corinthians 5:14-15
15. New Commentary on the Whole Bible: New Testament Volume; Copyright © 1990; Electronic Edition Files Copyright © 1998, Parsons Technology, Inc.; Tyndale House; Wheaton, Illinois

16. Ephesians 6:7
17. Matthew 5:41

Chapter 4: Workplace Ministry... What is it?

1. Colossians 1:27; 2 Corinthians 4:6-7
2. Some people believe these terms are from the Bible, stating Laity comes from the Greek word *laos* meaning people and Clergy from the Greek word *kleras*, which was used to distinguish certain people chosen by casting of lots for a special time and purpose. However these two terms are not used in the Bible to segregate ministry.
3. Mark 10:42-45
4. 2 Peter 1:2; Romans 1:1; James 1:1; Jude 1:1
5. Ephesians 6:7; Colossians 3:22-24
6. 1 Corinthians 10:31
7. For the word of God has sounded forth from you...but also in everyplace your faith toward God has gone forth, so that we have no need to say anything. (1 Thessalonians 1:8)

Chapter 5: Workplace Ministry A Challenge Environment

1. In the next section we will consider some of the dominant characteristics in your workplace.
2. The Christian Worldview gives the perspective how God created the world and called us to work; about why the world is in a fallen state and how God has made provisions for its solution; and how God is working in us, as we live in this world in its present state. Finally it shows God in control and moving history toward a final outcome. It is more than telling them what to do. It will affect our mind, will, and emotions.
3. Matthew 10:16
4. Hebrews 13:20-21
5. Psalms 23:4
6. 1 Peter 5:6-7
7. 2 Corinthians 12:9-10
8. 1 Corinthian 1:18-27
9. Matthew 5:14-16
10. 2 Corinthians 4:6, For God who said, "Light shine out of darkness"...
11. Why not consider how you are responding to the darkness around you at this time?
12. Philippians 2:14-15
13. Matthew 5:13; Colossians 4:5-6

Chapter 6: Workplace Ministry... Me?

1. This was one of the reasons why I began considering writing this book. It is my prayer and hope that in some small way it would be used to change this trend and help Christians see God's perspective of work and ministry.
2. 2 Corinthians 4:6-7
3. Romans 12:2
4. The section "Responding to Workplace Conditions" will go into more details.
5. Matthew 25:45 when doing this, we do it as though we were doing it for Christ himself.
6. Matthew 9:37-38; Luke 10:2; John 4:35-38; Romans 1:13; James 3:18
7. 1 Corinthians 3:6-9; 2 Corinthians 9:10
8. 2 Corinthians 1:4

Chapter 7: Having a Proactive Faith

1. Luke 6:28
2. Ignoring should not be confused with "overlooking"; there are times to overlook an offense and other times when problems need to be addressed correctly.
3. You can see this in the Four Gospels; when the disciples faced a problem it compelled them to run to Jesus for guidance and support. Jesus often used the occasion to instruct them in how to be on their guard and respond to a crisis at hand.
4. Luke 22:40
5. "Pray without ceasing." (1 Thessalonians 5:17)
6. Philippians 4:6-7
7. Romans 12:1-2
8. This is not some quick positive thinking technique which asks you to do certain things to get people to like you. Such techniques are superficial and do not address real problems, or work toward solutions.
9. James 3:13-18

Chapter 8: Rules of Engagement

1. Sande, Ken. (1997). *The Peacemaker*. Grand Rapids, MI: Baker Books; p.24
2. Matthew 5:44-47
3. Proverbs 23:7

4. Matthew 7:3-5
5. Philippians 4:5
6. Ephesians 4:15
7. As the offender-Matthew 5:23-24; as the offended-Matthew 18:15
8. James 1:19-20
9. Romans 12:21
10. Proverbs 25:21-22
11. Romans 12:18
12. Ephesians 6:9
13. Matthews 18:15-16 - while these verses apply within the church, a general principle of containment can be applied to situations.

Chapter 9: God's Bigger Picture
1. Some may use the purpose of a prophet to disagree with this statement. However, not everyone is called to be prophet, only a few.
2. 2 Peter 1:3-4
3. 1 Timothy 6:18
4. 1 Peter 1:6-7. Peter tells us that God is interested in putting our faith on display, not our gold/riches.
5. 2 Corinthians 5:16-18
6. 1 Peter 5:10
7. James 1:2-4
8. Gary Kosak email to the FCAP office staff, July 3, 2008
9. 1 Corinthians 13:12
10. Philippians 1:6; 2:13

Chapter 10: Making Our Connections
1. These two forms of the church are interrelated and one should not be emphasized at the expense of ignoring the other. Together they give us a balanced and full view of the church.
2. Ephesians 4:15-16; Colossians 2:19; 1 Corinthians 12:12-27
3. Exodus 33:14-16
4. Hebrews 11:13-16
5. This family identity has been established and is being built on Jesus Christ who is the same yesterday, today and forever.
6. John 14;17; Ephesians 1:13-14
7. Ephesians 4:3 - Actually, the original language gives the idea of our striving with all your energy to keep the unity that has been given to you.
8. In 1 Corinthians 3:11, Christ is said to be the only foundation and in Ephesians 2:20, He is said to be the cornerstone on which the building was aligned.

9. Some things they choose to stay away from- Eschatology, Spiritual gifts, Translations, and defending Christian leaders. They point people to Christ, and let God's Word be encouraging.
10. John 13:34-35
11. Hebrews 11:6
12. Walters, Delceta – email August 30, 2011

Chapter 11: The Church on the Move

1. Pope, Randy; *The Prevailing Church*; (Chicago, Moody Press 2002) pp 22
2. Matthew 16:14
3. Matthew 16:15
4. There are different interpretations regarding what the "rock" refers to. I believe it directly relates to the object of Peter's declaration, which is Christ himself - the rock.
5. In these verses Christ is said to be the cornerstone, Acts 4:11-12; Ephesians 2:20; 1 Peter 2:4-7
6. 1 Corinthians 3:11
7. Matthew 7:24-29
8. Like personality traits Christians bare the resemblance of needing forgiveness and offering forgiveness. They exercise a common trust in God to provide and guide them. They have the same hope in God. They come to God in the same way. They share God's love in the same degree.
9. Acts 17:2, 17; 18:4; 28:23; The word "reason" gives the idea of debating, using method of questions and answers.
10. Acts 2:32, 36; 4:11; 17:22-33
11. 2 Corinthians 5:20
12. Comparison between Roman 10:14 -declaring Christ by using words; and 1 Peter 3:1-4; declaring Christ by example, without words.
13. Romans 1:16; Refer to the Appendix- "*How Can I Know God*" for an explanation of the Gospel.
14. One of Christ's twelve disciples, Judas, never accepted His claim and betrayed Him. Peter himself would deny Christ three times.
15. A gate in that setting depicted an opening in a walled fortress where its leaders would sit to show their authority and control. At the gate they would guard and control activity in and out of it.
16. Jesus did say, be wise as serpents - avoiding dangers; and gentle as doves - not forcibly opposing (Matthew 10:16)
17. Matthew 9:36-38

About the Author

Paul grew up in a big family in Tampa, Florida where he enjoyed sports and recreation on the Bay. As a teenager he desired to enter vocational Christian ministry which led him to a ministerial and theological education at Florida Bible College in Hollywood, FL (Bachelor's Degree); L'Abri Fellowship in Huemoz, Switzerland; Biblical Seminary in Hatfield, PA; and Columbia International University in Columbia, SC (Master's Degree). In 1992 he became General Director of the Fellowship of Christian Airline Personnel, (FCAP). For more than two decades now, Paul has visited and worked with people both individually and in group settings in the workplace in North America, Europe, Asia, Africa, and the South Pacific. Paul and his wife Claudette serve together as a team in FCAP and live in the Atlanta, Georgia metropolitan area.

Preparing People For the Workplace

"God in Work" seeks to help people understand how their spiritual and professional life work as one. The Christian faith gives work its greatest purpose, and in the most practical ways. **Our training** gives people the opportunity to gain a greater perspective of a Biblical view of work and see how in practical ways this is lived out at work. This four-session training is facilitated in the following settings:

Business Settings

We provide trainings for employees, employee groups, and leadership that bring awareness and insight of God's design and purpose of work, by encouraging consistency and quality to how we do our work and bring value to our relationships at work.

Church Settings

Our training provides foundational tools and a game plan on how the people of your church, who spend 37% of life at work, can extend your church's ministry and mission. Our full training can be presented at churches and retreats. We also offer a condensed message that can be used for church services.

Christian Universities/Schools

 training is presented in classroom settings to prepare the current upcoming generations for how their professional life fits into bigger picture of bringing His influence and impact to the in the workplace.

Specialized Meetings

ning can be customized to address certain groups which deal ific issues and concerns regarding the workplace. Work ways of engaging amongst employee groups will be hrough the lens of a Biblical worldview.

Resources

provides articles as well as a **Weekly Thought** about the signing up you will receive it regularly. Testimonials for you to review.

ation on how we can accommodate you, please go to *work.com* or email us at *office@godinwork.com*